OSWALD AND I

MAURICE N. "NICK" MCDONALD
THE ARRESTING OFFICER OF LEE HARVEY OSWALD

Cover design, interior book design,
ebook design, and editing
by Blue Harvest Creative
www.blueharvestcreative.com

OSWALD AND I

Copyright © 2013 RMSW Press

All rights reserved. Except as permitted under the U.S. Copyright Act of 1976, no part of this publication may be reproduced, distributed, or transmitted in any form or by any means, or stored in a database or retrieval system, without prior written permission of the publisher.

This book is licensed for your personal enjoyment only. This book may not be re-sold or given away to other people. If you would like to share this book with another person, please purchase an additional copy for each recipient. If you're reading this book and did not purchase it, or it was not purchased for your use only, then please purchase your own copy. Thank you for respecting the hard work of this author.

Published by
RMSW Press

ISBN-13: 978-0615840239
ISBN-10: 061584023X

Cover photo and some photos in the photo gallery provided by the Estate of Maurice N. "Nick" McDonald.

Other photos provided through public domain use by University of North Texas Libraries, The Portal to Texas History, http://texashistory.unt.edu; crediting Dallas Municipal Archives, Dallas, Texas.

Photo of Nick McDonald holding one of Lee Harvey Oswald's revolvers licensed and used with permission of the Associated Press (AP).

Photo of Nick McDonald and Farris Rookstool, III used with permission and provided by Farris Rookstool, III.

TABLE OF CONTENTS

9
PREFACE: MAURICE N. "NICK" McDONALD

13
FOREWORD: FARRIS ROOKSTOOL, III

25
A NOTE FROM THE PUBLISHER: ASHLEY FONTAINNE

29
CHAPTER ONE: IN THE BEGINNING

34
CHAPTER TWO: THE ART OF GROWING UP

43
CHAPTER THREE: "GRAND-PARENTING"

53
CHAPTER FOUR: A MAN ON HIS OWN

68
CHAPTER FIVE: ME AND SALLY

77
CHAPTER SIX: CLOSE CALLS

89
CHAPTER SEVEN: THE PRESIDENTIAL PARTY ARRIVES

93
CHAPTER EIGHT: MOOD OF DALLAS

98
CHAPTER NINE: THE SHOOTINGS

103
CHAPTER TEN: THE ARREST AND CAPTURE OF OSWALD

108
CHAPTER ELEVEN: I GOT HIM, SARGE!

110
CHAPTER TWELVE: THE LINK

114
CHAPTER THIRTEEN: TWO CASES OF MURDER

117
CHAPTER FOURTEEN: ORDINARY COP

119
CHAPTER FIFTEEN: OSWALD SHOT

123
CHAPTER SIXTEEN: JACK RUBY

136
CHAPTER SEVENTEEN: MARINA IN LATER YEARS

143
CHAPTER EIGHTEEN: WARREN COMMISSION

156
CHAPTER NINETEEN: THE INFAMOUS ZAPRUDER FILM

160
CHAPTER TWENTY: THE PERILS OF PRESIDENTS

175
CHAPTER TWENTY-ONE: PROTECTING THE PRESIDENT

180
CHAPTER TWENTY-TWO: AWARDS AND HONORS

188
CHAPTER TWENTY-THREE: ROCKY MARCIANO

194
CHAPTER TWENTY-FOUR: HYANNIS PORT

199
CHAPTER TWENTY-FIVE: ROSE DAISY AND I

208
CHAPTER TWENTY-SIX: THE CLINTONS

212
CHAPTER TWENTY-SEVEN: 40TH ANNIVERSARY

217
PHOTO GALLERY

265
APPENDIX

DEDICATED TO...

The ordinary cop...the police officers willing to jeopardize their lives to protect and to serve others for the public good. They are their brother's keepers. They just do it!

My first wife and the mother of my children, Sally Lou Plyler McDonald. For her love and devotion during our twenty-five years of marriage, especially throughout the aftermath of the assassination and the arrest of Lee Harvey Oswald. Sally stood by me, helping me to cope with mental stresses.

My wife, Rose Daisy Brown McDonald, without her love and encouragement this endeavor could not be accomplished. I am very grateful for the love and support she has given to me over these twenty-seven plus years. I could not function, nor have the drive of completion, without her faith and prayers to go forward with this humble project.

"The credibility of theories can only be revealed and justified by the truth and established proven facts."

~ Maurice N. "Nick" McDonald ~

PREFACE

MAURICE N. "NICK" McDONALD

MANY BOOKS HAVE been written and movies made and viewed about the assassination of President John F. Kennedy. Nearly all have attacked the conclusion of the Warren Commission—which was that Lee Harvey Oswald was the lone assassin. Most of them criticized the Warren Report as a rush to judgment and finalization of the conclusion. Many of these conspiracy writers have theorized other suspects were responsible for the murder of Officer J. D. Tippit and the assassination of John F. Kennedy. They claim Lee Harvey Oswald was just a patsy in a grand conspiracy. To date, they have not produced any other suspects or a definite connection to any organization.

The public has been curiously receptive to conspiracy theories, from Oswald's defection to Soviet Russia, his support of Marxism beliefs, and his Pro-Communist philosophy embraced by Cuba's Fidel Castro's socialist form of government. These ties caused even more speculation.

More suspicions were raised when Jack Ruby silenced Oswald within forty-eight hours of the assassination. The Warren Report is mostly criticized by people who have never read it. Instead of the true facts, other matters have been focused on such as the Mafia, CIA, FBI and the Dallas Police.

Over the past four decades, many questions have been raised about the assassination. Very few answers have been provided by writers, telling of the documented evidences of those four tragic days, beginning with the assassination of President John F. Kennedy, November 22, 1963.

Sensational conspiracy claims may sell books and movies, but do not bring reasoning any closer to know and understand what really happened in Dallas during those terrible days. Examination of the direct evidence will resolve many issues and questions about the assassination of President John F. Kennedy and the killing of Lee Harvey Oswald.

This book is my way of informing the general public about my thoughts and my feelings as an ordinary cop; a police officer going about his duties, disciplined and trained to become an efficient and conscientious law enforcement official. In the beginning of my career, I was told criminals were out there and crimes were being committed every day. These criminals must be controlled for the public's good and safety. They must be penalized for their schemes of unlawful actions by detention and rehabilitation. The most successful system known by law enforcement is to apprehend and detain these menaces of society. The ultimate result is the prevention of crimes, and the protection of lives and property. After that, it's up to our court systems to define justice and to judge the punishment that equals the crime.

In my opinion, there is no such thing as a victimless crime. Someone is always going to be a victim, even the perpetrators themselves. Lee Harvey Oswald made victims. In the end, he also became a victim as did the self-professed vigilante, Jack Ruby.

John Fitzgerald Kennedy was not only President of the United States of America, he looked it. He was young, confident, clean-cut, and a happy man; a healthy symbol of might and power. Here was a man before the world personifying the mystique that his friends and aides had of him; confidence that Jack Kennedy would always win and move through life in handsome style.

In President Kennedy's inaugural address on January 20, 1961, these words have always stood out to me the most: "Let the word go forth from this time and place, to friend and foe alike, that the torch has been passed to a new generation."

But, in passing the torch, it was grasped too closely to the flame and new generations were burned, scorched, and singed by the actions of the FBI, the rushed judgment of the Warren Report, Vietnam, Watergate, Iran-Contra, El Salvador and by the Iraq weapons deal. The search and discovery of weapons of mass destruction by Iraq's Saddam Hussein produced no good effects. The U.S. government withheld the truth, gave only half-truths, spoon-fed, and piecemealed the American people on a need-to-know basis. That is all the new generations have.

The hope of those who came after, to find insight and wisdom in the task of continuing to explore the new frontiers, is forever lost to those in the future who fail to learn from the past.

Webster's New Collegiate Dictionary defines "*I*" as someone aware of possessing a personal individuality, and that is me. "Me" is defined as the objective case of *"I."* I do realize the my title does not follow the proper rules, but I wanted to emphasize *"I,"* because I was the one that survived the personal ordeal of November 22, 1963.

So, my writings became *Oswald and I*, with the emphasis on *"I."* What really happened? Did Oswald act alone? Do we have all the evidence? Was there a conspiracy? Who was involved? KGB? Cuba? Mafia? CIA? United States government officials?

I do not attempt to present new theories, nor support any other theories or to validate the complete findings of the Warren Commission Report. There is evidence that is puzzling and questions that will never be completely answered. I know what I did on that tragic day in Dallas to be true. I lived it. Come and live it with me....

FOREWORD

FARRIS ROOKSTOOL, III

ON NOVEMBER 22, 1963, one hundred twenty-eight minutes changed the world forever. The 35th President of the United States, John F. Kennedy, was assassinated in Dallas, Texas. Texas Governor John B. Connally was mortally wounded and Dallas Police Officer J.D. Tippit was murdered. Dallas Police Officer M.N. "Nick" McDonald arrested the suspect Lee Harvey Oswald for the murder of Officer J.D. Tippit within eighty-one minutes. A transfer of power occurred when Vice President Lyndon B. Johnson was sworn in as the 36th U.S. President.

In 1963, times were different. It wasn't a federal crime to kill the President. Four U.S. Presidents had been assassinated over the course of one hundred years before Congress took action. On August 28, 1965, Public Law 89-141 was signed into law making it a federal crime to kill the President. Our U.S. Constitution had to be amended. The 25th Amendment was ratified on February 23, 1967, which helped define the succession of the Presidency. In 1963, the Presidential limousine wasn't bulletproof. Police officers like J.D. Tippit and Nick McDonald didn't have the critical life-saving equipment such as bulletproof vests like we expect today.

One hundred twenty-eight minutes changed many lives, including mine, forever. On November 22, 1963, I was only two and a half years old. I was awakened from an afternoon nap when my mother was alerted of President Kennedy's assassination by a neighbor, Ms. Lela Bentley. My father was out of town on business and was flying back to Dallas Love Field airport. His flight was delayed due to all the air traffic held as a result of *Air Force One's* departure.

Later that evening, my family drove to Love Field airport to pick up my father and I can still remember the somber atmosphere in the terminal building. It was only a few hours earlier that Vice President Lyndon B. Johnson was sworn in as the new 36th President of the United States at Gate 28A and the body of President Kennedy was returned to Washington aboard *Air Force One*. I was too young to fully comprehend what had happened, but I knew it was something very serious. Looking back, it was difficult for me to imagine how a single event in my lifetime would define my life's work such as the Kennedy assassination. I know Nick McDonald felt that way his entire life. On one day, one arrest defined how he would be remembered for the rest of time.

On Sunday, November 24, just two days after the deaths of President Kennedy and Officer Tippit, my father and I watched Jack Ruby shoot Lee Harvey Oswald on our Emerson seventeen-inch black and white television. That was the first live television broadcast of a murder in American history. Ironically, my mother's former brother- in-law, Dr. G. Thomas Shires, M.D. was the attending surgeon who operated on Oswald and the doctor who pronounced him dead.

As a child, my father worked downtown and we would often drive past the Texas School Book Depository building. My mother always pointed toward the building and said, "That's the building where Lee Harvey Oswald shot President Kennedy." I always looked up at the sixth floor window. After the Warren Commission Report was published, I read the eight hundred and eighty-eight page summary report. I remember reading their official account of how Nick arrested Oswald.

It wasn't until 1969 when I was eight years old that I first saw Nick's face in Dallas Police Chief Jesse Curry's book the *JFK Assassination File*. In his book he published the evidentiary photos of the cut on Nick's face that resulted when he wrestled the gun away from Oswald. It was at that moment I truly appreciated Nick's heroic efforts.

Had Nick not been lightning fast in his response, Oswald would have killed him. Years later, Nick and I discussed why an innocent man who hadn't purchased a ninety-cent movie ticket would assault a police officer, and try and shoot him (in the presence of numerous Dallas Police officers) unless he was guilty of something.

In 1981, a year after Nick McDonald retired as sergeant after twenty-five years with the Dallas Police Department, I had my very first encounter with Lee Harvey Oswald. I was working at UT Southwestern Medical School as a medical artist and photographer.

In October, I became aware of an exhumation order granting permission to exhume Oswald's body. A British author named Michael Eddowes had written a book called the *Oswald File*. Eddowes book postulated that the real Oswald was switched in the Soviet Union with an imposter and the impostor returned to the US with his wife Marina. Eddowes theory was based solely on discrepancies in Oswald's height and official medical records. Eddowes persuaded Oswald's widow, Marina, to join him in the suit and allow Oswald's remains to be exhumed.

I contacted the assistant chief medical examiner whom I had worked with on a gunshot wound documentary and volunteered to serve as the official medical photographer for the exhumation. He granted me permission. The court ordered the exhumation of Oswald's remains, but the Dallas County Commissioner's Court objected to using county facilities. It was decided that Oswald's remains would not be examined at the Dallas County forensic lab, but rather at a private hospital (which ironically was where I was born). Since I had been previously approved to be present at the exhumation, I decided to go ahead and travel to Rose Hill Cemetery in Fort Worth, and witness history as they dug up Lee Harvey Oswald. A local newspaper photographer made an aerial photo of me looking at Oswald after they removed him from the grave. It ran the following day on the front page of the *Dallas Morning News*.

Nick always lamented how he captured the most famous criminal in America and yet not a single news photographer captured a photograph of them together. Years later, after Nick and I became friends, I would often tease him that even I had a picture taken with Oswald. He got a big laugh out of that.

In 1983, as the 20th anniversary of the JFK assassination approached, I applied to work for the Federal Bureau of Investigation. After passing the FBI's entrance examination, interview, and a lengthy background investigation, I was hired and sworn in the following year. I was beginning my law enforcement career shortly after Nick had retired.

In 1984, all of the original five hundred thousand pages of the FBI investigative files were returned to the Dallas FBI Field Office. They had been loaned to FBI Headquarters during the late 1970s for the House Select Committee on Assassinations investigation. When I expressed excitement about the return of the original JFK files, I was assigned the monumental task of inventorying the records to make sure all of the files had been returned. Over the next nine and a half years, I read every page of the classified JFK assassination records. To date I am the only person to have done so. With my ongoing interest in the Kennedy assassination, a new charitable organization was attempting to put an exhibit together in the former Texas School Book Depository. I called the organizations leader, Ms. Lindalyn Adams, and volunteered my services to the Dallas County Historical Foundation.

The Foundation was trying to raise capital to build a temporary exhibit focusing on the events that occurred that

November weekend. The exhibit was anticipated to last three years. From 1984-1989 I served as principle historical consultant to their organization. In 1988, during the 25th Kennedy assassination anniversary, anticipation grew quickly about the possible opening of a new exhibit titled: *The Sixth Floor Exhibit*. *The Sixth Floor Exhibit* opened the following year on President's Day, February 20, 1989. The exhibit transformed over time from a temporary exhibit into a permanent museum. It is now known as the *Sixth Floor Museum at Dealey Plaza*.

As I was driving to my office on May 25, 1989, I heard a local news broadcast on KRLD radio. They announced *The Sixth Floor Exhibit* had just acquired the "red upholstered chair, which was painted black after Oswald was arrested at the Texas Theater." Conover Hunt, Project Manager of *The Sixth Floor Exhibit*, indicated United Artists, who owned the Texas Theater, had donated it after it was requested. Upon hearing this broadcast, it immediately struck me that Hunt must have requested and received the wrong chair! I couldn't believe it. I recalled contradictory details in the November 22, 1963 official Dallas Police Department "Dear Chief" arrest report written by Police Sergeant Gerry Hill. The "Dear Chief" letter mentioned Oswald was "sitting three rows from the back...in the third seat." The Dallas Police Department also made an official investigation photo of Dallas Police officer Bill Anglin standing behind the fifth seat.

In 1965, the Texas Theater fifth seat was painted black during the theater's renovation.

On September 27, 1964, Nick had appeared on the CBS News program titled: *"November 22nd & the Warren Report."* He specifically stated that Oswald was sitting in "row three, seat number two" as he demonstrated the arrest to KRLD News Director Eddie Barker. To confuse matters further, Nick was later photographed standing in front of the black theater seat for the November 1983 *Life* magazine 20th special anniversary edition. I had to determine which chair was historically accurate.

In June 1989, I decided to write Nick McDonald a letter and introduce myself. I thought the best way to find out which chair Oswald was actually sitting in was to ask the man who arrested him. I needed to know for sure since there were conflicting accounts. I wondered if Hunt actually solicited and acquired the wrong chair. Nick promptly replied to my letter of introduction and inquiry. Nick explained to me that the black theater chair *was not* the chair Oswald was sitting in when he arrested him.

Oswald sat briefly in that chair when he had entered the theater. When Johnny Brewer pointed out Oswald to Nick from the stage, Oswald got up from the fifth seat and walked over to the second chair (same row) and sat down. Nick explained the photographer took his picture standing in front of the black theater seat for the magazine because the photographer thought it would be more dramatic—even though Nick informed him it was the wrong chair.

Hunt never contacted Nick to inquire which was the correct seat. Nick believed she had assumed it was the black chair simply because the theater painted it black. He closed his letter with an open invitation to visit him in Hot Springs, Arkansas.

I called Nick and thanked him for helping solving this historical mystery. I told him how much I would enjoy meeting him in person. The following month, I drove to Arkansas for a weekend visit. This was the beginning of a long and cherished friendship. Immediately, I loved Nick and his wife, Daisy. They were two of the greatest people I had ever met associated with the Kennedy assassination case.

Nick proudly showed me the uniform he wore on November 22. He showed me the numerous awards he received from all over the United States and then presented me with some buttons that were on his police uniform. Nick also gave me two 1964 silver Kennedy uncirculated half dollars that he had received after testifying at the Warren Commission. Within a few months of visiting Nick, the Texas Theater closed for good in December 1989.

The following year, with the Texas Theater closed and sitting empty and the talk of eminent destruction, I decided to contact a friend of mine who was Vice President of United Artists. I asked him if I could have the rest of the row of theater seats in which Lee Harvey Oswald sat. He said he would be happy to gift them to me. On March 15, 1990, United Artists gifted me the actual theater seat Lee Harvey Oswald was sitting when Nick McDonald arrested him on November 22, 1963 (row three, seat two).

I decided to drive to Arkansas with the original theater seat and have Nick autograph it. We had a wonderful time. We laughed about solving the historical mystery, and how we preserved a priceless artifact that was destined for wrecking ball.

The following year in 1991, Nick and I witnessed one of the worst perversions of facts in American history—the release of Oliver Stone's movie *JFK*. After its release, everyone wanted to contact Nick and me to ask us about the JFK assassination and offer their conspiracy theories. As a result of the movie, Congress was pressured to find a way to declassify and release all of the classified investigative files. In anticipation of a new law being passed, I was tasked with driving all of the FBI files from Dallas to Washington, D.C.—1,372 miles and twenty-six hours in a U-Haul truck. It was one of the most dangerous assignments of my FBI career. We dubbed it the "JFK Haul From Hell."

When we drove through Arkansas on our way to Washington, I couldn't help but think of my friend, Nick as we passed through his state. With the records safely returned to Washington, D.C., I found myself serving in a new role as the historical consultant on the FBI JFK Task Force. The following year, President George H.W. Bush signed Public Law 102-526 President John F. Kennedy Assassination Records Collection Act into law on October 26, 1992. After the declassification was complete, the FBI Unit Chief told me, "Farris, I think it's only appropriate that you be the one to drive them to the National Archives II in College Park, MD and complete their journey." I did and that is where the records reside today.

In 1993, as the 30th JFK assassination anniversary approached, it came quickly on the heels of the *JFK* movie. Nick and I found the interest in the Kennedy assassination was overwhelming. We received letters and requests from all over the world. I encouraged Nick to write his book. In December 1993, Nick mailed me his first rough draft. I was proud of him and told him generations to come needed to know his story. Nick said, "Farris, I just want my book in school libraries across the country so kids can learn the truth of what happened on November 22nd and who knows maybe it might encourage one of them to pursue a career in law enforcement like I did."

Writing the foreword to Nick's book completes my five-year effort to honor the November 22nd heroes who helped make the arrest of Lee Harvey Oswald possible. Heroes are ordinary people who do extraordinary things in difficult times. Though Nick always signed his name as "Captor of Oswald," Nick always made sure that others were given their proper credit for helping him in the arrest. I made it a personal cause to help honor and recognize these men for their monumental contributions to our American history.

In 2009, I assisted the Dallas Police department with the restoration of a 1963 Ford Galaxie. The vehicle was painted to resemble J.D. Tippit's police car. The car was donated to the Dallas Police department and restored as a tribute to the memory of all fallen police officers. On November 22, the entire Tippit family gathered at Tenth Street and Patton Avenue at the site of where J.D. was killed. I placed the replica police car in the exact location using crime scene photos and measurements. Privately, I carefully explained the events of the tragedy to them and this was the very first time they had gathered as a family at the crime scene.

I submitted a request in 2009 to Dallas Police Chief David Kunkle to honor Mr. Temple F. Bowley with the Dallas Police Departments highest citizen award—*The Citizen's Certificate of Merit*. Bowley was the citizen who was driving west on Tenth Street and discovered the fatally wounded body of Tippit lying in the street. Bowley immediately got out of his car and used Tippit's police radio and called for help. It was Bowley's broadcast that alerted Nick (who was standing in front of the Texas School Book Depository at 411 Elm Street) that his friend and fellow officer had been shot. On November 22, 2010, forty-seven years later, Dallas Police Chief David Brown honored Temple F. Bowley with the Dallas Police Department's *Citizen's Certificate of Merit* for his actions of coming to the aide of Officer Tippit.

The following year in 2011, I submitted a request to Dallas Police Chief David Brown to honor Johnny C. Brewer, former manager of Hardy's Shoe Store with the Dallas Police Department *Citizen's Certificate of Merit*. On November 22nd at 1:38 p.m., Brewer heard a KLIF news broadcast on his transistor radio "that a police officer had been shot and killed near the 500 block of West Jefferson." Brewer looked up after hearing the broadcast and saw Oswald standing in the foyer of his shoe store acting suspiciously. Brewer followed Oswald as he entered the Texas Theater. Brewer stopped and asked Texas Theater employee Julia Postal to call the police. He suspected this man might have been involved in the shooting of Officer Tippit. Brewer stood guard at the theaters fire exit door and waited till police arrived. Nick McDonald and fellow officers pounded on the theaters fire exit doors and Brewer let them in. Brewer pointed out to Nick McDonald where Oswald was sitting in the back of the theater. Nick always credited Johnny as the man most responsible for assisting him with the arrest.

On November 21, 2011, the night before Johnny was awarded with the Dallas Police *Citizen's Certificate of Merit*, I presented him one of my signed Nick McDonald 1964 Silver Kennedy uncirculated half dollars. I felt Nick would want Johnny to have it. It brought tears to both our eyes. Johnny told me that he never got to thank Nick for what he did that day. Johnny said Nick would always be his hero. The last time Johnny saw Nick was on November 22nd when they were together on the stage at the Texas Theater. Forty-eight years later, on November 22, 2011, we presented Johnny with the police commendation on the very stage Johnny had shared with Nick. Johnny and I both carried our silver half dollars in our pockets as our personal silent tribute to Nick.

In 2012, I helped honor the memory of J.D. Tippit with a Texas Historical Commission Marker at the scene of J.D.'s murder. When Dallas Police first awarded Temple Bowley with the *Citizen's Certificate of Merit*, a local news reporter asked why Officer Tippit had not been honored or even recognized with a historical marker at the scene of his murder. Most people don't realize the murder of Officer Tippit was what made the capture of Oswald possible within eighty-one minutes of the assassination of President Kennedy. I informed the news reporter to count on me for assistance. With that pledge, I prepared the official one hundred and nine page historical narrative recommending the marker to the Dallas County Historical Commission as well as Texas Historical Commission.

I appeared on local television and within a day, a citizen stepped forward and pledged the funds needed to produce the state marker. Next I traveled to Austin to pledge my support of the marker and on January 27th I witnessed the unanimous vote by the Texas Historical Commission alongside Johnny Brewer. The Texas Historical Commission marker was dedicated close to the 49th anniversary on November 20, 2012. For the first time, my friend M.N. McDonald's name was credited on a state historical marker as the arresting officer of Lee Harvey Oswald. Generations to come will also learn about the men who greatly assisted Nick in the arrest—the names of Temple Bowley and Johnny Brewer are also credited for their actions on November 22nd.

November 22, 2013, commemorates the 50th anniversary of the assassination of President John F. Kennedy, the wounding of Texas Governor John Connally, the killing of Officer J.D. Tippit, and the arrest of Lee Harvey Oswald. Sadly, Nick is no longer with us. Nick passed away January 27, 2005 from complications from diabetes at the age of seventy-six. There are some people you wish would never die. Nick was one of them. He was one of the greatest men I knew. My life was much richer having had Nick McDonald as my friend. Police work was Nick's life and he loved it more than anything, except his wife Daisy.

I miss him greatly. I choose not to think that Nick is no longer with us. I prefer to say he went on what law enforcement officers call a "double six"—he ended his tour of duty.

I hope future generations will come to know my friend Nick through this book and will love and admire him as I do. He lived his life to the best of his ability, served and protected our country and our community, and was kind to his fellow man. I wish we had more people like Nick McDonald.

Nick, the country will be forever grateful for your service and you will never be forgotten. God bless you and thank you for being my friend.

Farris Rookstool, III
Historian & Former FBI Analyst

Farris and Nick

A NOTE FROM THE PUBLISHER

ASHLEY FONTAINNE

IT IS A rare event when you are fortunate enough to be a part of releasing a piece of history to the public. My publishing imprint, RMSW Press, falls into that category. While conducting research for an historical novel I am currently working on, a chance meeting took place in Hot Springs, Arkansas in April of 2013. My mother, who works at a retirement village in Hot Springs, arranged for a group of seniors to meet with me and share their memories of times long past for my book. I was excited to meet a roomful of people who are part of the greatest generation the world has ever seen.

One of the guests that day was Daisy McDonald, the widow of former Dallas Police Officer Maurice N. "Nick" McDonald. After the meeting, she approached me with questions about my experiences in publishing. We immediately hit it off and talked several times over the course of the next few weeks. One day during a long conversation, she offered me the unimaginable: she wanted RMSW Press to publish her husband's work.

Mr. McDonald had written his memoirs about how his life was impacted from the moment he arrested Lee Harvey Oswald at a movie theater in Dallas. He typed the first chapter in 1993 and the final one at the end of 2004. Sadly, Mr. McDonald passed away in 2005 and his heartfelt story sat unread inside a thick binder, along with all the photographic memorabilia he acquired over the years. It was his dying wish to see it in print.

It is with humility, thankfulness, and a sense of duty and honor that I bring to the world the memoirs of Mr. McDonald. This book catalogues his thoughts and feelings before and after the arrest, ending with his participation in the 40th anniversary proceedings in Dallas. For those of you seeking yet another chapter to add to the copious amount of conspiracy theories, you've chosen the wrong book. This is the life story of one ordinary man thrown into an extraordinary situation and how that one moment impacted his life forever.

To the family of Mr. McDonald—thank you all for entrusting me with this opportunity to make his last wish a reality.

    Ashley Fontainne
    Author/Owner, RMSW Press, LLC

"I expect to pass through this world but once. Any good therefore that I can do, or any kindness that I can show to any fellow creature, let me do it now. Let me not defer or neglect it, for I shall not pass this way again!"

~ Author Unknown ~

1

IN THE BEGINNING

THE BUDDING FLOWERS bordering a lush, green yard that surrounded a modest, white painted house were slowly being awakened by the first day of spring, March 21, 1928, in the small paper mill town of Camden, Arkansas.

In the stillness of that early morning, a sharp, resounding slap applied to the tiny buttocks of a newborn was echoed throughout the spacious rooms. God's sweet breath of spring had once again breathed the gift of life into another material, but spiritual, being.

Dr. Jameson had been alerted and had rushed to my grandmother's house and to a corner bedroom where my mother lay in her labor. He was struggling feverishly, perspiration beaded on his forehead, in an effort to aid my mother with a difficult delivery.

My father, Thomas Biddie (Bid) McDonald, was a roughneck laborer in the booming oil fields of south Arkansas and northern Louisiana. My mother, Beulah Lee Womack McDonald, had returned to her mother's to await my arrival. I was evidently overanxious to exit the comfort of my mother's womb so there wasn't time for cranking up a Model A by my grandfather for a trip to the hospital.

My grandmother, Laura Rich Womack, told me in later years that on that day she had secretly adopted me in her heart to replace the grief she suffered in the loss of her youngest son, who died of typhoid fever in the fall of 1927, just a few short months before my birth. My uncle, Dauphin, was only seventeen at the time and had contracted the fever on a high school band trip to Hot Springs, Arkansas. Mama (my grandmother) said to me, "The hardest thing in life to overcome is for a mother to lose a child before her own death."

I was the youngest of two boys. My brother, Charles, watched over me during my early childhood and was my mentor. To him, I must have been quite a pest. I attempted to follow him every place he would go. He was five years my senior and I had been much too young to be with him and his friends. Dar (I couldn't say Charles) would try to sneak off from me when he wanted to be with his friends. I remember on one occasion while we were visiting relatives in Pine Bluff, Arkansas, I attempted to follow Dar and his friends. In the shadows of darkness, I became confused and disoriented. Suddenly, the sun fell like a rock and I was in total darkness.

Just as suddenly, my mother missed me and went outside, looking around the house and up and down the streets. I was nowhere to be found. She became frantic and called the police to help search for me.

After searching for what seemed hours, I was found wandering alongside an angry, rushing river. With a broad smile, a friendly but concerned motorcycle policeman picked me up, and with a gloved hand rubbed my snow white cropped hair with tender affection. Lifting me, he placed me astride his thundering motorcycle. As he mounted his machine behind me, he pulled my tiny body tightly to his and told me to hold on with both hands to his arms that were outstretched clutching the chrome handlebars. Roaring through the streets, he returned me safely to my mother's arms. Her tears of anxiety became smiles of relief and happiness, as only a mother could know.

My first contact with this tall, imposing, but gentle policeman, had a lasting effect of admiration and respect. Deep down, that brief encounter and memory of this kind policeman greatly influenced my ultimate decision to become a career police officer. I wanted to be like him; friendly and kind, but firm.

During my preschool years, we were living across town from my grandparents. I wandered away from my mother's view once again. While she was busily raking leaves and wasn't looking, I headed out for grandma's house. I was very attached to my grandparents and they in turn had bonded with me. Their love for me was bountiful and they owned and operated a neighborhood grocery store which, to me, had the largest candy supply in the world. When we visited they would spoil me rotten with their love and affection, and allowed me to explore the candy cases and choose whatever assortment of candies I desired. I filled my pockets until they bulged, and my face beamed with happiness. Who could resist a cute, towheaded boy with a smile as big as the outdoors?

On my first attempt to get to grandmother's house, my absence was noticed immediately. My mother telephoned my grandfather (papa) and asked him to be on the lookout, as I was probably headed that way. Papa got into his old Model A Ford and started for downtown.

Papa found me wandering on the street going in the general direction of his store. He stood me up in the front seat of his Model A Ford and drove me to their grocery store. My eyes began to sparkle with anticipation of flavorful ice creams, all kinds of candy, and cold drinks. Papa called mother and told her I was with them and I was okay. They assured her I was safe and sound and convinced her I should spend the day with them since I was already there. I was loved, pampered, and spoiled thoroughly that day. When Papa and Mama took me home, and with the pleading to my mother from Mama, my corporal punishment was suspended and I was sent to bed after a lengthy lecture and scolding.

A few days later, I tried my venture once again. This time my experience was totally different. I somehow managed to get as far as the drugstore downtown and stopped on the corner to rest on the curb. Knowing me from previous visits, the druggist, Mr. Patrick, brought me an ice cream cone and wanted to know where I was going? In my three year old talk, I answered, "goin' see Mama and Papa, at th' dore!" At about the same time, my grandfather drove up. Scolding me he put me in the car, making me sit in the seat. Instead of taking me back to his store, he drove me home to my mother.

She was standing in the yard, anxiously waiting for us with an angry, determined look on her face. *I'm really in for it now!* Mother could see my cotton top head just barely visible over the Model A's dash. Papa lifted me from the car seat, looking down and avoiding mother's eyes, and said sorrowfully, "Here, Beulah, I guess you will have to do something with him this time, but don't be too hard on him!" With Papa out of sight, the stinging switch that reddened my tiny legs and the warm tears that streamed down my puffy cheeks, convinced me that my wandering trips to my grandparents were over. I had learned my lesson for good.

During my fifth year, mother gave birth to another boy, Gerald Thomas McDonald; his middle name "Thomas," after our father. Gerald was born prematurely, and his short life only lasted a mere thirty-two hours. This tragedy brought about an emotional strain on my mother and a challenging change in the relationship between my mother and my father. Mother wanted the baby very much and the loss was unbearable for her.

While mother was still in the hospital, recovering from the ill-fated birth, baby Gerald was quietly buried in a small plot. The grave was outside of the curbed lot that had been reserved by my grandparents, where they had laid to rest their youngest son, Dauphin. This was also where they would be buried.

When mother learned where her parents had buried Gerald's body, she was hurt and felt rejected by her family for not allowing the baby to be buried in the family plot. The tiny grave was marked by a small metal frame with only the sketchy information printed on plain paper. After thirty-five years, Gerald's little grave was marked with a proper headstone. My mother instructed me to see to it that the stone was bought, inscribed, and placed at Gerald's grave site.

2

THE ART OF GROWING UP

WHEN I WAS six my parents moved to El Dorado, Arkansas. My father changed jobs requiring him to relocate. He was employed by an oil company in south Arkansas as a driver of a gasoline tanker.

I started my first grade year of school at Yokum Elementary. I found out very quickly how to make a nickel at my young age. I noticed there were two older boys who bullied a few of the smaller boys and took their lunch money. A couple of boys in my class came to me and asked me to protect them from the bullies. They would give me a nickel. I wasn't big for my age, but I guess I displayed a fearless attitude and wasn't going to be intimidated by anyone. I agreed to protect them and the very next day they tried to take their money again. I got between them and I stood up to the bullyboys. I gave one a black eye and they both scampered out of sight. I was rewarded with five cent Fudgsicles from my benefactors. The word must have gotten out because none of the boys were ever taken advantage of or bullied out of their lunch money again.

Even here in El Dorado, I tried to be as big as my brother Charles. On one July 4th, he and his friend, Wayne Lindsay, were out in the backyard shooting fireworks. My longing to be a part of their schemes and activities caused an unfortunate accident to happen. I wandered out into the backyard and was looking for them. My brother leaped out from his hiding place behind the garage and started shouting frantically for me to go back. I ignored his warnings, thinking they were trying to avoid me again.

Before I could interpret his warning and realize the immediate danger, excruciating pain gripped my left leg. Blood gushed from a gaping wound where glass from an exploding firecracker penetrated the calf muscle of my leg. They had thrown caution to the wind and placed a firecracker under a glass fruit jar to see what would happen. I looked at my leg in horror. Screaming, I stood frozen to the spot. Charles ran to me as fast as he could run. Quickly removing the glass, he wrapped a rag around my leg and applied pressure to stop the bleeding. He then lifted me up to his shoulders and started running with me piggyback to a doctor who lived nearby.

The doctor happened to be home on this holiday. Taking me from my brother, he placed me on the kitchen table and performed a hasty operation that probably saved my leg. That prominent scar is still a memory of those daring boyhood days and of exploding firecrackers under glass. I am amazed at how children survive to adulthood when they are faced with injurious and unexpected dangers in their day-to-day lives.

In my third year of school, my mother divorced my father. At that time I could not understand what brought about the separation. Charles and I accepted the divorce with unanswered questions. In later years, I learned it apparently developed from the unexpected death of my little brother, Gerald. Differences came about between them and I remember heated arguments and disagreements. Happiness and harmony were not guests in our home.

Mother moved us to another part of town, away from our father, and I changed schools in the process. I joined the Boy Scouts of America and began to learn about different things by earning merit badges, and performing a variety of tasks. As a Tenderfoot, we were required to hike fourteen miles round trip. I made the hike, but not without a price. Boy, oh boy, was I ever a tenderfoot! My feet became one big blister and I was laid up for two solid weeks with infections. I'm sorry to say that ended my scouting days.

I also acquired my first job, a door-to-door salesman selling magazines from my little *Liberty* canvas bag that hung from my shoulder. "Hello ma'am, would you like to buy one of these magazines? I have *Liberty* and *Saturday Evening Post* for only a nickel!"

I was unsuccessful in selling magazines. Without realizing it at the age of ten, I was an environmentalist. Collecting scrap metal became a way of life. Pulling my little red wagon with sideboards up and down the alleyways, I began collecting scrap metal to sell to the scrap dealer to earn extra spending money. By the end of the week, I tried to collect at least one hundred pounds. The dealer was paying one cent per pound for scrap iron and finding a hundred pounds made me richer by a whole dollar. One day while checking behind an auto repair shop, deep in the grass I discovered an old, broken down car engine. It was like finding a gold mine. By the time I had dismantled the engine, the parts weighed nearly four hundred pounds. I hit a four dollar bonanza.

With the aggressive war in Europe, and Germany invading and occupying country after country, our own country was slowly becoming a nation eager to recycle. Our leaders were trying to stay out of the war, but we had to try and be prepared. The irony of it all was at that time our country was selling our scrap metal to Japan.

The scrap collecting business began to slow down and scrap became harder to find. I needed another source for spending money. My grandmother Laura bought a second-hand bicycle for my thirteenth birthday. Now I was ready to try my hand at being a paperboy with wheels and my very own paper route. I found a vacated paper route with the *Arkansas Democrat* morning paper. I had the grand total of sixty-three daily and Sunday customers. There were no problems in delivering the papers until one Sunday morning.

That particular Sunday edition had added pages and each paper seemed to weigh a ton. With my cloth bag bulging, I somehow managed to struggle home. It was already daylight and I knew that my customers were wondering why their Sunday paper was not yet delivered. My mother met me at the door and could see that I had been struggling. She volunteered to help me with delivering them. We divided up the papers, mother walking alongside my bicycle and taking turns throwing papers like a seasoned paperboy.

Now a single parent with two boys to raise, mother worked as a saleslady for a millinery shop. In her spare time at home she was a dressmaker and worked many hours late into the night. To augment her income, she rented a spare bedroom to waitresses. Mother would do anything to make an honest living and she instilled this work ethic in her two boys. In our spare time, we collected empty milk and Coke bottles, and even wire coat hangers for resale to stores and dry cleaners. It was necessary for us to do these things to survive and to have a little something extra that we could share with mother.

Hard times fell on us when mother lost her job at the millinery shop. After an exhaustive effort, she was offered a sewing position with the W.P.A. (Works Progress Administration; [earlier, Works Project Administration]) working long hours for very little pay.

My mother had a grand idea of operating a boarding house. She found an empty house for rent just down the street and we moved immediately into this larger house that had extra bedrooms and included a full bath upstairs. This was perfect for taking in boarders. She could set a beautiful table, even if the fare was only corn bread and red beans. Mother managed to keep three or four roomers and during the lunch meal extra plates were set to accommodate workers who seemed to drift in from nowhere.

Evidently, the word got around praising the wonderful food at a reasonable price—just fifty cents for all you would want to eat including dessert. Even the morticians from the funeral home next door graced her table, nattily dressed in their traditional black suits. I remember sitting at the table across from them and all I could do was stare as I imagined all types of ghoulish stories about undertakers. I wondered how anyone could sit down to a beautiful meal after working on dead bodies without getting sick to their stomachs. I thought to myself, *Did they wash their hands and change clothes? Or, did they come straight from the embalming room? And, what was that awful smell coming from their clothing?*

I asked mother what was that terrible odor and very quietly and discreetly she said, "Oh, that's a chemical called formaldehyde. They use that in preparing dead bodies. Promise you won't say anything about it, they might hear you. You would embarrass them!" I shook my head dumbly.

Times were beginning to get harder. The workers started losing their jobs and stopped coming for lunch altogether. The roomers moved out and, much to her chagrin, mother finally had to give up the boarding house. At the age of sixteen my brother Charles left home and went out into the world to make his way. Mother decided, now that her oldest son had left home, she would move to Shreveport, Louisiana and start all over again.

It was now 1940 and I had completed the sixth grade at Hugh Goodwin Elementary in El Dorado. Mother sent me to my grandparents for the summer, while she settled herself in a new town. I was to stay with my grandparents for only the summer, but as school's opening drew near my grandmother convinced my mother that it would be better if I stayed with them and attended school in Camden. Mother found a job and was working peculiar hours at a defense plant near Minden, Louisiana where they made ammunition for the big guns. She hesitated but finally gave in and agreed reluctantly. She knew I would be home alone most of the time and not supervised properly.

Camden High School was just across the street from my grandparents' grocery store and their home, and I only had a short walk. The store was always crowded at lunchtime by the school kids. At noon time, I rushed back to the store to help with the onslaught. My job was opening the soft drinks and collecting a nickel, the price of a soft drink. My grandmother set up a little gas stove at the rear of the store and cooked hamburgers and hot dogs. Hamburgers cost fifteen cents and the hot dogs were ten cents. Mama made up her own sauce consisting of mustard, onion and pickle relish to put on the buns. That special mixture still tantalizes my taste buds.

I participated in all the sports my high school offered and was proficient enough to earn school letters in three of them; football, basketball, and track. The following fall season of football during the rough and tumble practice scrimmage, a couple of my fellow players fell on my left leg, consequently breaking the small bone in my lower leg. While recuperating with my leg in a cast, I tearfully watched my team practice without me. Grandmother's front porch was just high enough for me to get an unobstructed view of the football field. For all practical purposes that injury ended my short career as a football player.

After my disappointment, grandmother suggested that I become a member of the high school band, as had her son, Dauphin. She kept a set of his drums put away, deep in her closet. I assumed she wanted me to follow in his footsteps and play the drums, but she told me that I could choose any instrument. I tried the trumpet, but soon discovered I was more adaptable to the baritone horn, and earned second chair of the brass section.

I was pledged to one of the popular fraternities organized in high school. This was just another way of being socially accepted in the school and around the town. I was now part of the "in crowd." My life was filled with school activities and loyal friends. I even acquired a nickname. One of the guys didn't care for my first name and he told me he was going to call me "Nick," from the word nickname. From that day forward, I was "Nick." A nickname seems to become part of one's personality, and the name has a way of attaching and becoming a part of you.

My nature was friendly and easy going and not the aggressive type. At a pledge party the members decided to stage a boxing bout among the pledges. One classmate and fellow pledge was considered a tough guy and the largest boy in our eighth grade class. At random, the members picked me to be his opponent. He donned the gloves first and was eagerly waiting for a challenger, making a show of sparring and jabbing empty space. I guess it was an attempt to dissuade any challenger.

I tried to subdue and ignore my inner fear as the gloves were being laced to my small hands. Extending the huge pillows of soft leather in front of my body, I attempted to imitate the proper stance of a prize fighter. As I moved to his left, he rushed at me with glaring eyes, swinging a wild haymaker. I dropped my chin to my chest, closed my eyes and waited for the blow. At the same time, I drove my heavy gloved right hand into his face. The rushing air above my head caused my hair to stand on end. He suddenly fell back, and I could see the gushing red from his nose splattering his surprised face. It was all over with that single punch. Everyone crowded around me with glee and raised my arms in victory.

At the same time, I was glad it was over and sorry I had hurt him by bloodying his nose. I offered my handkerchief to help stop the bleeding, but he turned away. I knew that I had not only bloodied his nose, but I had injured his pride. After his hurt feelings subsided, we became closer friends.

After proving my courage to the other pledges, they elected me to be their sergeant at arms. The title meant I was to defend the honor of my fellow pledges against the pledges of the one competing fraternity. Unknown to me, a contest was proposed that the sergeant at arms of both fraternity pledges would engage in a fight.

One day after school, the pledges of both frats gathered behind the stadium on a hill overlooking the girls' softball game in progress. It was just a boy thing in asserting masculinity or to be macho in front of the girls. Harry McMichael and I wrestled and rolled around on the ground not really wanting to hurt one another. As if by plan, we tightly gripped clinching scissor holds with our legs around one another's bodies and were at an impasse. Each of us unwilling to admit defeat in our playful battle, it was declared a draw. Shaking hands, we went our different ways without feelings of animosity.

My summers were spent in Shreveport with my mother. I found summer jobs and worked as a soda jerk in Walgreen's drugstore on the main drag, Texas Street. Within a short time, I became manager of the soda fountain. When it was time for school to start again, I wanted to return to Camden and continue to live with my grandparents. I wanted to be with my friends and classmates for the coming school year. Mother knew in her heart I would be better off with them. She did not want to disrupt my life with a change of schools and be among strangers at a new one. I promised mother I would be with her again next summer.

3
"GRAND-PARENTING"

AFTER MUCH DISCUSSION, it was finally decided that I would live with my grandparents and go to school. It was a sad occasion for my mother. On the other hand, I was looking forward to exciting experiences, anticipating new adventures, and opportunities to explore other avenues. I never thought I would miss my mother or that she would miss me. I was too young to realize the real emotional impact of our separation. In the back of my mind, I knew my mother and I would be together in the summer, and with the expectation that sooner or later we would make a home together again.

I never really had a real father figure to help shape and mold my boyhood. As an adolescent, I needed guidance by an authority figure and my grandfather, Charlie Womack, provided that for me. He was not stern, but a firm and gentle man. You could tell by the tone of his voice he meant what he said when he said it.

In the wintertime, we would sit for hours around the store's potbellied stove. Papa would tell story after story about his teenage years, his army life, and how he met and married my grandmother, Laura.

He volunteered for the U.S. Army during the Spanish-American War and was sent to Tennessee for encampment and training. His army buddy and tent-mate, Will Rich, was from Tennessee and had ten brothers and sisters. Will's baby sister, Laura, was seventeen and unmarried. When Will showed a tintype photograph of her, Charlie asked and got her mailing address. He wanted to write and get to know her better. This started a long letter writing relationship. They discovered they were from similar backgrounds and both raised on a farm. The only difference was that Charlie's father was a farmer and Laura's father was a Presbyterian preacher.

After the battle for San Juan Hill was fought and the war was over, Charlie was discharged and returned to Ouachita County, Arkansas. His best friend, Joe Galleon, and he got together and formed a "Magic Lantern" show. George played the guitar and Charlie played the fiddle. They had a one-horse covered carriage with a small stage on the back where they could sing and play for small community gatherings of south Arkansas, northern Louisiana, and east Texas. They would use a little schoolhouse or a small church to show their "Magic Lantern," reflecting pictures on a wall of people, places, animals, and things most had never seen before. They didn't charge admission, but they did accept contributions. With a grin he said, "Sometimes they would give us biscuits and molasses or invite us in to a supper!"

After Papa made enough money with the "Magic Lantern," he took a train to Tennessee to finally meet Laura. They were already in love with each other from the letters. Papa went to the Reverend, Mr. Sib Rich, and asked for Miss Laura's hand. They were married and Papa brought Miss Laura on the train to south Arkansas as Mrs. Charles H. Womack.

Charlie's father gave them a piece of his land with a house already built on it for a wedding gift. To start farming, Papa had to mortgage the land for $50 to buy a pair of good plow mules. When the next good crop came in, they were able to pay off the mortgage.

Their first born was my mother, Beulah Lee Womack. They were blessed with three other children; Ruby, Raymond, and Dauphin. As they grew, they worked on the farm alongside my grandfather and my grandmother, sun up to sun down. Saving as they worked, Papa was the first person in the community to buy a Model T Ford so he opened a small gas station alongside the main road of the farm. By the time their youngest, Dauphin, was 16, Papa sold a few acres of the farm and the little gas station. He bought a grocery store with a house next door in the town of Camden, Arkansas.

My grandfather liked to sit around the fire. He would get out his old fiddle and play familiar tunes like *Red River Valley, Turkey In The Straw* and *Home, Sweet Home*. Mama would get out her Jew's harp and join in. I would keep time by tapping my feet and clapping my hands, and tried to sing the words along with Papa. The old wooden floors of the grocery store would bend and creak with the music.

I will never forget the times that Papa took me to the circus. When he learned that a circus was coming to town, he would take me down to the railroad station to watch the elephants and other wild animals that were unloaded from the long line of railroad cars. Later, we would go downtown and watch the parade of the horse-drawn colorful circus wagons with the animals pacing back and forth in their cages. The calliope, with its steam whistles, filled the air with boisterous music. There were painted clowns of every description. They were dressed in oversized shoes and colorful costumes; cartwheeling, skipping along with brightly colored balloons, giving out candy, and teasing the young children.

Beautiful ladies, scantily clad in their tights, rode high on top of the huge heads of the majestic elephants following one another trunk to tail. It was one of the most exciting, thrilling sights I had ever seen. Papa loved the circus, but he pretended he just wanted to take his grandchildren to see the spectacular events. He enjoyed every moment of the three-ring circus. It was "the greatest show on earth."

As I grew older, Papa took me out to the woods and along the Ouachita River banks. He taught me how to shoot with his .22 caliber rifle. We saw a cottonmouth water moccasin snake swimming toward the bank of the river. Papa handed me his rifle and told me to try to shoot it. Taking aim, I shot at the snake, but cut a hanging vine in two. Taking another shot, I hit the snake, but it kept swimming to shore. I took several more shots. The snake finally made it to the bank but was not moving. We went down to the edge of the river and found that the water moccasin had expired. I had hit him six times, but he kept on swimming.

My next learning experience was a lesson in right and wrong. When I helped out in the grocery store, I had access to the cash drawer and to my grandfather's money sack, which was mostly silver and a few small bills. One day I helped myself to a roll of quarters. I had no idea what I was going to do with them. I left them in my jacket pocket and forgot all about it. My grandmother was checking my dirty clothes, and when she picked up my jacket the roll of quarters fell to the floor. Mama called out to me, "Marty, where did you get these quarters? Did you take them from the store?"

With a guilty look on my face and a shrug, I replied, "Yes, ma'am!"

"Without asking?"

"Yes, ma'am. I'm sorry."

My grandmother's way of punishing me was by pinching and twisting the flesh on my side and arms with her long fingers. It hurt like the dickens.

"You take those quarters and give them to your grandfather and tell him what you did. Shame on you!"

I would have preferred a real beating than face my grandfather. I took the roll of quarters and handed them to Papa. With tears in my eyes, I said, "Papa, I took these quarters from your store. I'm sorry and I promise I will never take anything ever again."

"Did you tell your grandmother about this?"

"Yes, sir! She found them when they fell out of my pocket and she pinched me real hard for taking them. She even made me bring them to you and tell you what I had done."

"Why did you take them?"

"I don't know. I guess I just wanted a roll of quarters to carry around in my pocket."

Papa said, "I'm not going to punish you; I want to know one thing. Am I ever going to be able to trust you again?"

"Oh yes, Papa! I will never take anything that does not belong to me ever again. I promise."

This was the best lesson of right and wrong to ever learn. It has stayed with me throughout my life.

Early in my teens, my grandfather spoke politics every time an election was going to be held—county, state, or national. He was a true Democrat. I sat in his store for hours and listened to his likes and his dislikes of different party lines and platforms. His favorite president was Franklin Delano Roosevelt.

I remember one year he entered politics and ran for county coroner. He had held the office of justice of the peace for years. I was a witness to many of the couples coming by at all hours to be joined in matrimony. The year he ran for county coroner I went with him on several occasions to all types of gatherings, from barbecue cookouts, to potluck suppers. Any place a crowd gathered, he attended and gave speeches, asking for their vote and support. My job was to hand his printed circulars and campaign cards out that detailed the changes he would make if elected.

The election primaries were held in the hottest month in Arkansas—July. On election night it was always hot and muggy. We all gathered on the county courthouse lawn to wait for the election returns to come in from the ballot boxes. A huge blackboard was erected on the speaker's platform. When a ballot box was counted, the election judges chalked the number of votes from each box beside the candidate's name.

My grandfather always had a big red bandana to fan and wipe the sweat from his face and neck with. Then he would take off his wide brim straw hat and fanned with that. My grandmother was more resourceful than Papa and me. She brought a lawn chair from home and a church fan with an image of Jesus on one side. When that didn't help, she would raise up her signature apron and fanned with that.

Papa watched the board and mentally added the votes of his opponent. I stood on tiptoe to look over the crowd trying to see the big blackboard and the figures being tallied. Around 11:00 p.m. Papa turned from the board displaying the election figures and said, "Let's go home folks! We've lost the coroner's job. My opponent has won."

It wasn't that wide a margin, but it was enough for Papa to admit defeat. He never ran for an elective office again.

During the Presidential campaign of 1960, my grandfather and I discussed the candidates according to their individual accomplishments. Even though Richard Nixon had been a vice president, he had no outstanding political attributes to his credit. Nixon's appearance and smirky attitude displayed an expression of doubt and insincerity, especially when he appeared to be highly nervous. He was not a convincing leader as John Kennedy had demonstrated in life and in Congress.

We both discussed the fact that Kennedy was a Roman Catholic, but we were convinced that he would run the country and not take orders from the Pope in Rome if he became president.

We agreed that the country needed fresh blood and a young vibrant man to run our country. John F. Kennedy was our man. Of course, we both voted for him. My grandmother lost her battle with liver cancer in 1961. She was the matriarch of our family and the glue that held us all together. She was my second mother, and I loved her dearly. My grandfather, was my father figure; my confident; my teacher. Most of all he was my *hero*.

Papa lived long enough to tell and brag to anyone who would listen that his grandson, Maurice, had captured and arrested the accused assassin of President John F. Kennedy. I was happy that Papa could be proud of me. I have regretted that my grandmother did not live long enough to know what I had accomplished. But I knew she was proud of me up in Heaven.

One of the hardest things I ever had to do was to be one of Papa's pallbearers. My grandfather requested that his six grandsons carry his coffin at his funeral. It was very difficult for me. He had raised me as his son and I looked up to him as my only father.

Tears dampening my cheeks, I remembered how he took me by the hand and led me honestly and truly in the right direction. Now it was my turn to help carry this wonderful man. My beloved grandfather, Papa, who had carried me so many times. Only now I was taking him to his final resting place.

During my absence from my mother in Shreveport, her girlfriend had been dating a man in the Air Force. He had a buddy that wanted to meet her and have them go on a double date. My mother hesitated but finally agreed. They all went out to dinner and a show. He was a real gentleman, polite and courteous in every way and she really liked him.

Mother called me at grandmother's and told me all about him. She said his name was Norman Calderwood, he was in the Air Force, and from Maine. I asked if she was serious about him.

She said, "Yes, we are getting very serious and may get married soon! He is due to ship out to India any day now and he wants to get married before he leaves. We are going to get married this weekend." Since my brother, Charles, had joined the army and I was living with my grandparents, I told her it would be the right thing to do.

Norman Calderwood was stationed at Barksdale Air Force Base in Shreveport. In civilian life he was a lobster fisherman from a tiny island fishing village, thirteen miles off the rocky coast of Maine. They were married, and a week later Norman shipped out for India. He told mother to gather up her things and go to Maine and wait for him.

On her way to Maine, mother stopped by my grandparents to tell everyone goodbye. She had pre-shipped most of her belongings and had only a couple of suitcases. Mother only stayed two days and she was off on her journey to New England. At my age it seemed she was going to the ends of the earth. When she did finally arrive at Vinalhaven Island, she followed Norman's directions and caught a taxi to take her to Norman's parents' place. She had no idea she was going to the other end of the island.

She asked the taxi driver if he knew where he was going and he assured her he knew the place. The driver turned on a dirt road and drove to the bottom of a mountain and said, "Well, this is as far as I can go!" He put her suitcases on the ground and pointing, he said, "See that little trail through the trees?"

"Yes, but I have on high heel shoes. I might stumble and break a heel! What do I do then?"

"Just keep walking and you'll find their big, yellow house on the shore."

"Where in the world am I?"

"You're at the base of Tiptoe mountain along Crockett River shores. Keep going down that trail and you will find the Calderwood's."

Mother was careful as she walked down the spruce-lined dark trail. She was dressed to the nines in a form-fitting black dress complete with open-toed high heels, and a black hat. She finally made it down to the shore, and just like the taxi driver said, there on the edge of Crockett River was the Calderwood's house.

She was greeted at the door by Norman's mother, Gen, and his father, Frank O. Calderwood. Gen was a short, pudgy, round woman with a cheerful face. Old Frank had a slightly brown, long gray moustache. His stature was short and bent from hauling lobster pots from the ledges of the ocean floor.

They welcomed mother with open arms. She was so relieved to finally get there. She went upstairs to her room, sat on the edge of the bed, and opened the window ever so slightly and lit a cigarette, careful to blow the smoke out of the window. She did not want her new in-laws to know she smoked, even though Frank had a pipe in his mouth 24/7, so it seemed.

The war finally ended and Norman came home to his bride. They began their lives in a small, rented cottage with a view of Crockett River. They had no plumbing or electricity, and water was carried to the house from the free running spring down a slope of their hill.

I was too young to fully understand my mother's reason for marrying again, leaving me behind and moving two thousand miles away. Secretly, I felt that mother had abandoned me, when in reality, years before I had abandoned her. I had a genuine "pity party." Then my high school sweetheart broke up with me. I thought, *I'll show everyone. I'll join the navy and they will all be sorry for leaving me.*

I was only seventeen and my grandmother had to become my guardian. The navy would not allow me to enlist unless a parent or a guardian signed my enlistment papers. My grandmother was concerned about me leaving and joining the service at such a young age and tried to talk me out of it. I explained that I had to leave and be on my own because there were innuendos by my Uncle Raymond that I had been mooching off his mother and father long enough.

She apologized for her son's resentment toward me and reluctantly signed the papers. I was on my way.

4

A MAN ON HIS OWN

LEAVING HIGH SCHOOL in January 1946, I enlisted in the United States Navy for a two year hitch. At the ripe old age of seventeen I was through with school and my friends forever. I had great expectations and aspirations of being a man; a man on his own, thinking that I could make it in a completely different world than I had known as a child.

In my youth my grandfather told me of his adventures of his army life during the Spanish-American War. I remembered being spellbound by his stories. In the summer he wore short sleeves and his arm was tattooed in bold, beautiful colors with a waving American Flag. I greatly admired my grandfather, and was awed by his bravery. How proud he was displaying his tattoo for all to see. It was the mark of a man for me. I kept saying to myself, *If my grandfather can bear the pain with honor, surely I can do the same.*

As a prerequisite for being a man in the U.S. Navy, one must be tattooed. All sailors are tattooed, aren't they? On my first liberty from boot camp I strolled the streets of San Diego among the sea of white sailor caps. I was trying to decide which tattoo parlor to select to disfigure my arm with a ship's anchor.

For a five dollar bill, I was now a man—a navy man! I kept thinking how proud my grandfather was going to be. Man, oh man, was I ever wrong.

Everyone is classified as a seaman first class when they enter the U.S. Navy. After boot camp, everyone is classified as seaman second class. The reasoning for this was so no one was ranked lower aboard a seagoing vessel. When the boatswain blew his pipe (whistle) and spoke over the ship's PA system for "all hands to report topside and man your brooms, sweep fore and aft throughout the ship," every seaman immediately stopped what they were doing, reported and grabbed a broom.

On other occasions, we were ordered to join the deck crews to chip, scrape, and paint the metal deck and sides. The chip hammers and wire brushes were special tools designed for scraping the metal, cleaning paint bubbles, and rust spots. The paint used was a yellow zinc rust preventative applied to the chipped and scraped bare metal. They would lower you by block and tackle lines while seated in a boatswain's chair, which was nothing but a tiny board resting on a line (rope). In the navy a rope was called a line. When you were finished, yellow paint would be splattered over you and your dungarees.

Boot training completed, I had a ten day leave and returned to Camden and my grandparent's home. I strutted about the town, showing off my new uniform with an egotistical attitude in a vain effort to make the guys envy me and attempting to impress the girls. I was the handsome, uniformed "big shot navy man."

My grandfather was not impressed with my tattoo. He scolded me for having such a foolish thing done. I said, "You have one. Why can't I have one like you?"

He replied, "I was young and foolish and have wished many times that I could have it erased from my arm. Just because I was foolish in my youth gives no reason to copy me."

After my short leave, I was assigned to Camp Shoemaker, a shipping and receiving station near San Francisco. When I arrived, I learned that just across the back fence was a German prisoner of war camp. At first, I thought they were soldiers waiting to be transferred, just as I was, until I tried to have a conversation with one of them. He could not speak English and just grunted. From all outward appearances, they were treated like any other soldier.

Along with eight hundred sailors, sailing with us were also six hundred soldiers, (mainly ex-convicts released from Leavenworth prison convicted for all types of crimes.) Most were to be a part of the Occupation Forces in Japan. With other raw navy boots, we would be reassigned to a ship in Hawaii.

The ship journey from San Francisco to Hawaii was an experience I will never forget. It took us seven days and our transport was a Merchant Marine vessel, the *Marine Wolf*. The saddest sight I will ever remember was standing on the fantail of the ship steaming for the Hawaiian Islands. A huge banner was draped over the Golden Gate Bridge that read *Welcome Home Boys!*

And here I was leaving the good old USA for parts of the world unknown to me. Tears came to my eyes and chills ran down the length of my back. I was leaving and they were coming home. I was a frightened, young teenager as I'm sure they were in the beginning. But now they were much older and much wiser in their new role of fatigued battlefield veterans.

During our third day out to sea from Treasure Island, I was finally able to overcome my sea sickness. When I pulled the midnight watch, a mess cook came around with hot coffee and cookies. I took a bite of the cookie and a sip of coffee, and that was all it took for me to lose my own cookies over the side. After that, my sea sickness was gone forever.

I tried to eat the terrible food served to us, but the ship's cook had no imagination. Cold cuts, noon and night, and a conglomeration of what they laughingly referred to as powdered eggs for breakfast. In the dining hall, there was no seating. You were required to stand at long tables and attempt to keep your food tray from sliding back and forth down the table. The lurching of the rolling ship was fighting the lashing waves of the dark ocean. In the distance, the sound and the vibration could be heard and felt from the twin screws heaving out of the water as the ship plowed through the heavy seas. If you were an "old salt" you could weather the sea, but you were sure to be sickened by the terrible food.

A few of the ex-convicts were protesting the food and took it upon themselves to break into the ship's stores and took whatever supplies of food and cigarettes they could carry.

When the burglary was discovered, the captain restricted the ship and would not permit anyone to leave the ship on our arrival at Pearl Harbor. When we had docked, it took the captain about six hours to discover the perpetrators and recover most of the stolen goods.

After that episode, we were allowed to leave the ship and continue to our appointed destinations. Once again, I reported to a shipping and receiving station, Aiea, located near Pearl City. Waiting for my permanent ship assignment, I was given menial duties of a mess cook and cleaning the officer's club in Honolulu.

New orders were a welcome sight, and I was assigned to the *USS Coasters Harbor* (AG-74), an electronic repair ship. I left immediately and boarded the old "74," which had been docked in Pearl Harbor, near the half-submerged *Arizona*. As I boarded my ship, I gave the customary salute to the duty officer on deck and to Old Glory flying on the fantail. I faced the *Arizona*, and for a moment I gave a hardy salute and said a silent prayer for the men who lost their lives on that tragic day, December 7, 1941. The following day we sailed for the Marshall Islands.

Steaming from Hawaii, we arrived at Kwajalein Atoll, a part of the Marshall Islands, and picked up additional stores and supplies. Anchoring offshore, tenders made round trips from the island to our ship with supplies. We loaded them onto the ship. We formed a bucket brigade along the gangway ladder and passed the boxes and crates up the gangway to the deck, stacking the stores on a pallet. When full, the cable winch hoisted and lowered it into the ship's hole for storage. I was thankful I was not assigned in the hole where the temperature was one hundred twenty degrees plus. It took us two days to finish.

We continued on to our destination, Bikini Atoll, and made anchor in the beautiful blue bay of the tiny island. I learned through scuttlebutt we were going to be part of *Operation Crossroads,* a large task force. Many ships and thousands of men had been selected to participate in the atomic bomb testing at Bikini.

Arriving offshore of Bikini, we anchored a mile from the beach. During the preparations for the two explosives testing, we were allowed to go ashore on Bikini every other Thursday for recreational beer drinking. This became a ritual of 15T scrip beer and softball games combining into fights with fist and bats as tempers flared in the torrid heat of this "tropical paradise." The redeeming factors, if you could call them that, were the beautiful, sandy beaches and the blue-green inviting waters surrounding this previously undisturbed, little island.

We were told the first atomic bomb test would involve the dropping of the bomb and detonating it above the island and target ships strategically anchored around Bikini Atoll. My ship, *USS Coasters Harbor,* was anchored seventeen miles away from the first atomic bomb test. The crew was ordered topside, and the only safety instructions were to turn our heads away and shield our eyes from the blast and the flash from "the bomb." The devastating explosion was deafening to the ears, and the flash of light blinded the sun. Next came the tidal waves that rolled and tossed the anchored ships as if they were toys in a bathtub. The mushroom cloud was there but not as imposing as the second bomb test.

The second atomic test would be an underwater detonation. Again, we were anchored away from the island, but this time we were much closer. We were only twelve miles from the blast. We were all just a bunch of navy guinea pigs. The effect was as the first, only this time after the flash of light, I turned and I could see what appeared to be one of the larger ships turned on end at the edge of the mushroom cloud. I learned it was the battleship *Alabama*. The *Alabama* and the *Arkansas*, among others, were now on the bottom off the shore of Bikini. The designated target ship was the battleship *Nevada* and it had been painted an unmistakable bright orange.

On returning to anchorage off the coast of what was now the remains of Bikini, we could see that some of the target ships were left almost intact. Other ships were now lying on the sandy graveyard bottom, among the wreckages from the first blast. Standing on the decks of our ship, you could almost feel the unfiltered radioactive waves floating in the atmosphere.

The invisible, ever present, death dealing menace appeared to be harmless, but in experimental testing of exposed subjects, willing or not, how can it be determined? In my case, I was never informed one way or another.

A crew member, John Smitherman, on board the USS *Allan M. Sumner* (Destroyer 692) that was nineteen miles away reported that after the Able bomb was dropped, he and other firemen went aboard the carrier USS *Independence* without any protection of any kind. The *Independence,* one of the target ships, was on fire from the Able shot. Smitherman was sent to fight that fire without any protection. The only thing he was wearing at the time was a pair of shorts, a pair of sneakers, and a turned down sailor cap.

"We fought the fire aboard the *Independence,* one hour on and two hours off. I did that three times. When we came on board the landing craft that was waiting for us, we had to go through and be monitored by Geiger counters."[1]

Several men in white coats, covered from head to toe, went aboard the carrier with Geiger counters. Smitherman stated, "I was just seventeen and none of us had the slightest idea of what a Geiger counter was, or what radiation was because that was never explained to us at any time...we watched the Baker shot from a ship about nineteen miles away from the explosion, and a mist from the mushroom fell on the deck of our ship and sand fell on our deck, and also little pieces of metal and rocks. We tried to wash off as much as we could. The mushroom cloud stayed in the air for almost two days—we could see that."[2]

Smitherman later developed lymphedema, a blockage of the lymph system that causes legs and arms to swell; he had both legs amputated. On September 11, 1983, he died of cancer of the colon, liver, stomach, lung, and spleen. He had claimed compensation for radiation damages. The Veterans Administration turned his claim down seven times.[3]

My ship was subjected to the same radiation fallout, only we were seven miles closer to the Baker shot. We sailed back to the lagoon of Bikini and anchored within twenty-five yards of a captured German cruiser that had been targeted, and was still afloat withstanding both blasts.

Almost fifteen hundred nuclear devices have been detonated since 1945. Approximately two hundred fifty of these were American atmosphere nuclear weapons tests. It was estimated forty-two thousand men and women participated in *Operation Crossroads*.

Thousands of military personnel in war and post wartimes have witnessed the United States use of the Atom bomb and were exposed to mushroom clouds, dust and debris, with no protection. These men and women have witnessed test series spending their tour of duty on ships or stationed on bases on or near irradiated lagoons in the Pacific. They were ordered deck-top or to beaches to watch these tests, such as shots Able and Baker at *Operation Crossroads*. They slept on the ship decks exposed to atmospheric fallout from these U.S. nuclear tests. Without knowing, they bathed in contaminated lagoon waters.

The men and women who were involved in the testing and use of nuclear weapons while serving in the U.S. military are known as Atomic Veterans. Many of these Atomic Veterans are now profoundly ill and live in expectations of an early death. Many of their children are genetically affected. They and their families have had to bear emotional and financial costs alone. Their government claims the tests did not affect the health of these former servicemen, and has refused them compensation or medical help in most cases, citing they were exposed to no more radiation than they would get in a chest X-ray.

These servicemen and women lived and worked on contaminated soils, ships, and water for extended periods. Plutonium and radioisotopes could have entered their bodies throughout the dusty air they breathed, and the food and water they consumed.

"Limited compensation and some medical care has been approved to civilian populations in the Pacific, who are recognized to have extraordinary illnesses, cancer, premature death, and birth defects, as a result of exposure to fallout from American weapons tests. Japanese victims of Hiroshima and Nagasaki continue to develop new symptoms and continue to die from their exposure years after the bombing. They too receive limited medical care and some U.S. financial aid. But this help has not been received by the majority of U.S. Atomic Veterans. Why have American Atomic Veterans and their families found it extraordinary difficult, if not impossible, to receive assistance from their own country? What made these veterans immune to the radiation hazards that so seriously affected the Japanese Marshallese?"[4]

The following are excerpts of the Congressional Hearing on *Operation Crossroads* held in Washington, D.C. on December 11, 1985. Lieutenant General John L. Pickitt, director of the Defense Nuclear Agency and the executive agent for the Department of Defense Nuclear Test Personnel Review (NTPR) program made this statement to the committee: "Decontamination of personnel who visited the target ships is not significant issue with respect to doses actually received. Between July 25, 1946, only about 4,900 personnel boarded target ships. These personnel were scientists retrieving data from instrumentation, damage inspections teams, and accompanying radiation safety monitors. Most of these personnel had extensive experience as a result of their previous work on the Manhattan safety and decontamination procedures....

There is no reason to assume that the approximately 9,000 people (21% of the Crossroads participants) who actually boarded the target vessels received any additional exposure as a result of inadequate personal decontamination.... We have great sympathy for any veteran who is suffering from disease or disability. At the same time, however, we have an obligation to assure that the doses assigned to individuals reflect, as accurately as possible, both the historical facts and the best available scientific methodology."[5]

The Atomic Veteran is left with few sources of assistance as his own government has turned away and denies his claim for care and help. Despite President John F. Kennedy's wish, as he announced the end of atmosphere testing to the nation in July 1963, that, "The loss of even one human life or the malformation of even one baby...should be concern to all of us..." The Atomic Veteran is still waiting for expression of that concern.[6]

On the bottom of the lagoon of Bikini Atoll lie twenty-one vessels of war, many the pride of the victorious U.S. Navy of World War II. The wrecks lie in about one hundred eighty feet of water. The aircraft carrier *USS Saratoga*, flagship of Bikini's sunken fleet, battered by two nuclear explosions, sits upright on the lagoon bottom. The top of the carrier's superstructure is only twenty feet beneath the surface. The flight deck is about ninety feet down. Many of the servicemen who witnessed the nuclear test cried when she sank the day after being rocked by an underwater nuclear blast with the explosive power of twenty-three thousand tons of TNT.

But no one wept for the Japanese battleship *Nagato*, a prize of war that the navy also sacrificed to the Bikini test. The *Nagato* was the Japanese flagship and command ship for the attack on Pearl Harbor, now resting upside down on the bottom near the *USS Saratoga*.[7]

Hopefully, devastations such as these will never happen again in this dangerous nuclear world.

Settling down to our duties, we looked forward to the weekly mail boats bringing mail from home and movies for the ship's crew. Receiving a variety of movies was a real rarity. We were stuck with the movie, *It's A Pleasure*, starring Sonja Henie. She was a famous Norwegian ice skater turned movie star. She won the Olympic Gold Medal three times, 1928, 1932 and 1936. The projector and movie screen were set up on the fantail of the ship. As this was the only movie that was available for our ship at the time, we watched it over and over.

Each time it was shown, the ship's company anticipated the dialogue and repeated the script lines along with the actors. On every trip of the mail boat we tried to get a different movie without much luck. Using signal flags to the other ships, we offered to trade for their movie, any movie. Finally, a ship agreed to trade their old western movie for the beautiful Sonja Henie.

Another recreational scheme I thought of was renting high powered binoculars to my shipmates. The binoculars came from my storeroom and for a five cent pack of cigarettes from the ship's stores, they could have a look-see for one minute. There was a hospital ship anchored one thousand yards away and it was loaded with female nurses. On bright, sunny days, they washed their "undies," hung them out to dry in the fresh, ocean breezes, and sometimes sunbathed in skimpy bathing suits on the ship's deck. The guys got a real thrill out of watching the activity of the nurses. These men had not seen a woman since Hawaii.

My little escapade only lasted a few minutes before my boss, Lieutenant Shanklin, shut me down. Taking the binoculars and chewing me out properly, he left shaking his head while trying to conceal a small grin. After our mission was completed we left the Marshall Islands, towing a hotel barge used as living quarters for scientists, engineers, and construction personnel. After the atomic tests and their jobs completed, other means of transportation were used to take them back to stateside.

The empty hotel barge was massive. It was a heavy, cumbersome object restricting progress of our ship, causing it to struggle against the rolling seas, and reducing our headway by three knots.

At last we reached Hawaii for a brief stopover. This was our first sight of real civilization in over ten months. The very first thing I did was to go to the nearest Honolulu cafe and order a real American hamburger and a whole quart of sweet milk. For months, we had nothing but powdered milk and powered eggs. The sight of fresh milk and the smell of grilled hamburgers was a king's banquet to me. A two day stopover in Honolulu was much too brief, but there was a feeling of joy as we continued struggling with barge in tow heading stateside. Our destination: San Pedro, California.

After thirty days towing the barge, we delivered it and left the *Coasters Harbor* to be decommissioned and placed in mothballs. She performed her duties in wartime and post wartime gallantly. It was reported that a few of the target ships that remained afloat had been towed to the San Francisco Bay area where they tried to decontaminate them without success. They finally took the contaminated ships out to sea and had them sunk.

I was transferred to North Island Naval Air Station in San Diego Bay. My new assignment was storekeeper at the VRU-3, U.S. Navy Bomber Squadron. I was responsible for supplying and re-ordering spare parts for the aircraft assigned to our squadron. The squadron was made-up of approximately ten officers, pilots, and forty enlisted men with ten aircraft. The aircraft were SB2U Vindicator, more often called vibrator by the pilots who flew them. They were navy bombers that served as scout bombers and dive bombers during World War II aboard the aircraft carriers *Lexington, Saratoga, Ranger,* and the *Wasp.*

I was probably the youngest man in the squadron and took a lot of kidding from the men. One day, I was busy working in my storeroom, when Lieutenant Brodowski, one of the "hot shot" pilots, came by and stuck his head in the half door and said, "Hey Mack, do you have any skyhooks on hand? We need to hoist my engine out."

I looked at him quizzically. "What does a skyhook look like?"

He said impatiently, "It's shaped like a regular hook, son!"

I searched the parts room to no avail. I replied meekly, "Lieutenant Brodowski, sir, I don't think we have skyhooks."

"Well, I guess you will have to order one ASAP. I need that engine out and repaired, or I'll lose my flight pay!"

I went to the parts catalog and was searching when I looked up and saw a crowd of men standing in front of the door. They were all smiling as if I was the butt of a joke.

"What's so damn funny?" I scowled at them. They all started walking away.

An old seasoned chief petty officer said, "Well, son, think about it. How would you ever hook a skyhook to the sky? The lieutenant gottcha good!"

I smiled and laughed with my pranksters. Still smiling, I asked, "Have any of you guys seen my left-handed monkey wrench?" Laughing with me, they realized I could take a joke as well as answer with a joke.

I HAD JUST turned nineteen and I was still too young to frequent bars and nightclubs. My sources of entertainment consisted of amusement parks, movies, and the local roller skating rinks.

At that time, navy regulations did not allow enlisted personnel to wear civilian clothing on the base, but we were allowed to wear civvies after leaving the base. When I got off the ferry (commonly called the nickel snatcher since the fare was only a nickel) from North Island Naval Air Station to San Diego, I changed into my civilian clothes. After changing, I took the "A" train to Long Beach to spend my liberty at the Hippodrome Skating Rink where I met a beautiful, blonde California girl. When the rink closed, we boarded a bus and I took her home.

Every liberty, I went to the rink looking for her. If she was there, we skated until closing time and once again I would see her home with a quick, good night kiss. Quickly, because I knew from other times her father would click the porch light.

One Saturday night she failed to show up as we had planned. I went to her home and the darkened house was empty. My pretty California girl had just vanished with her parents to places unknown. I had a "thing" for her. We were just skating partners and close friends, never lovers. She was a sixteen year old school girl and I was a nineteen year old navy man.

I remember returning to the naval base and waiting at the ferry terminal for the return trip. A lonely jukebox was standing in the corner softly playing *That's My Desire* and *To Each His Own* by Frankie Laine and Ted Weems' arrangement of the whistling tune *Heartaches*. These melodies reminded me of my California girl. Even today, those long forgotten melodies re-surface from the recesses of my mind and take me back to those wonderful, youthful days.

At the end of 1947, I had completed my two year navy tour of duty, receiving an honorable discharge, World War II Victory medal and the Good Conduct medal. I took my $300 mustering out pay and left San Diego and returned home by Greyhound bus. Along the bus route, we were traveling through Dallas, Texas. Dallas seemed quaint for such a growing city. There were no expressways on the journey through the quiet residential streets reaching the outward bound highway.

Looking back, I never dreamt that someday I would return and become part of Dallas' modern history with their busy freeways, expressways, and shopping centers.

Returning to Camden, I resumed my formal education and entered college. I enrolled at Arkansas State Teachers College, Conway, Arkansas. The college is now The University of Central Arkansas. I became an active member of the "in crowd," and was pledged to one of the popular Greek fraternities Phi Lambda Chi. I can't say that it helped scholastically, but it did widen my social standings on campus.

5

ME AND SALLY

WHEN I RETURNED to Camden from college, I met Sally. My grandmother decided to play Cupid and had been telling me of a pretty girl who was visiting her sister who lived next door. It was a meeting I will never forget.

Early one morning my grandmother called me to breakfast. I got out of bed, sleep walking into the kitchen clad in my rumpled pajamas, hair uncombed, scratching, and yawning. I couldn't have looked worse if I tried. Just a few feet away stood this beautiful girl, Sally, using my grandmother's telephone. I stood motionless, blinking with sleepy eyes, trying to clearly see this vision.

My grandmother said, "Nicky, I would like you to meet Sally. She is the girl I have been telling you about."

I answered with an embarrassed, "Hello."

Sally smiled and answered with a girlish laugh, "Hi."

I excused my appearance and quickly backed out of the kitchen. After finding my robe, I returned. To my dismay, Sally was gone.

From that day forward our infatuation with each other seemed to weld our hearts into deep, true love. After eighteen months of dating and discovering our mutual interests and dreams, we finally became engaged on New Year's Eve 1950. The war in Korea was escalating into a full-fledged conflict and the USA was totally committed. I was an active member of the Naval Reserve and knew it would be only a matter of time before I was recalled. I had to make a decision. We wanted to marry and I knew if I was called for active duty we would be apart most of the time. I could vividly remember how sea duty made me lonely during those never ending days and nights.

Many nights I would just stand at the rail and look at the moonlit horizon, wishing I were someplace else. Glancing down, I watched the sides of the ship slice through the immense ocean. Tiny sparks of phosphorus radiated energy from the ship's path through the water, and sprinkled a glow for just an instant. This effect resembled billions of sparklers gracing the darkened sky. The silent movement of the ship failed to disturb the quietness of the night. The full moon and twinkling stars, reflected by the deep, dark waters of the ocean, gave me a feeling of unbearable loneliness; a feeling that I was the only person left in the world. I knew that it would go away if it were possible to reach out and touch someone you loved.

December 29, 1950, I enlisted in the United States Air Force and the very same day, I received my honorable discharge from the United States Naval Reserve. After celebrating our engagement on New Year's Eve, I left for Lackland Air Force Training Center. Having previous service, I was awarded the rank of PFC (private first class) and it was not required of me to go through the normal routine of basic training. Large numbers of men were enlisting in the air force and the overflow had filled the capacity of the base. Most had to be quartered in army tents. Tent life and my processing and indoctrination took twenty days.

To decrease the influx and overcrowded population of service personnel at Lackland, we were flown out to the different service schools at air force bases throughout the country. I was assigned to Radar Operator's School, Keesler Air Force Base, Biloxi, Mississippi. When I arrived at Keesler Air Force Base, it was like going to a different planet. It felt as if I had been placed in the middle of a basic training camp. There were raw enlistees all over the place.

Biloxi was yet another world. Gambling was wide-spread in every business place in town. Slot machines were everywhere from service stations, bus stations, and drugstores to even the smallest cafes to the best restaurants. Hard liquor was sold openly all over the town. This was 1951 and gambling and the sale of liquor was illegal in Mississippi.

Even the local police were on the take. An incident was told to me by one of my fellow air force buddies, who had been arrested for a minor infraction. Before he was released, he had to pay a $250 fine and the arresting cop $100 to replace his uniform. The arresting officer accused him of tearing his shirt and trousers when he arrested him. My buddy denied he had even touched this "dirty cop." I learned this was standard operating procedure for the Biloxi police.

After my indoctrination at Keesler, I was assigned to Radar Operator's School for the short six week training period. It was limited to the basics of proficiently operating the radar scope. This required identifying blips on a tiny, round green screen. When the bright, sweeping beam enhanced an image displayed on the screen, your responsibility was to calculate the distance and speed of the blip. The radar operator then communicated this information directly to a person standing behind a two-sided, plastic plotting board. This person's duty was to mark and track the blips' location on the board noting location, distance, direction, and speed. A signal device was used in friendly aircraft that would register on the radar screen. If an aircraft did not reflect this device, it was classified as unfriendly. This caused an automatic challenge to the unidentified aircraft.

The radar training required knowledge in the component parts of radar monitoring equipment, as well as the round-shaped covering scanning tower and signal scanner housed within the radar tower. During this training the CQ (charge of quarters) came in my barracks while I was still sleeping and shouted, "Private McDonald, are you in here?"

Yawning in a sleep garbled voice, I answered, "Sir, yes sir! I'm over here."

"Get dressed. There's a young lady at the front gate asking for you." I quickly jumped into my fatigues and ran to the front gate.

Sally was waiting in a taxi. I was speechless seeing her here in Biloxi. We had agreed to be married after I had been reassigned to my permanent base. This was much earlier than I had expected. Breathless, I took her out of the cab and we hugged and kissed. "What happened?" I whispered.

"My sister's husband is in school here and they have a small apartment. I thought I could stay with them until we were married. Anyway, I missed you and want to get married and be with you now."

I explained to her that I had duty that day and I could not possibly leave the base until that afternoon. "How in this world can we get married this soon? I only have three dollars to my name."

Sally said smugly, "I have thirty dollars and that's more than enough to get married. You can use your three dollars for the marriage license."

"Okay. You go to your sister's and I'll try to get a three-day pass."

I tried all day to get a pass but was repeatedly turned down. I didn't know where else to turn. I finally resorted to a conspiracy with my barrack sergeant literally for a cover-up. I explained I was getting married and I had been unable to obtain a three day pass until the weekend and asked him if he would cover for me at the 10:00 p.m. bed check. He agreed to roll up a blanket and place it in my bunk. I promised him faithfully I would report at 6:00 a.m. for the morning muster.

Completing my duties for the day, I rushed to Sally and explained I had made a deal with my barrack's sergeant to cover for me overnight. Sally was anxious to get married that day because we had to be married to stay with her sister.

We started trying to make the arrangements. That meant going to Gulfport Courthouse before closing to get the license. We began calling JPs and preachers. After rushing to the Gulfport Courthouse before closing and getting the license, a Baptist minister agreed to marry us back in Biloxi in his church study. Now we were all set! Rushing to the church, we arrived in quick order, but my nerves were on end. I was in my dress blues and Sally was in a simple yet beautiful light blue dress—very appropriate for the occasion.

I kept the wedding band in my deep uniform pocket and while nervously repeating the vows, I fumbled around and finally found it. The ring was wrapped and hidden among pocket lint. Picking off the fuzz and repeating after the preacher, I said, "With this finger, I thee wed. Excuse me. I mean with this ring, I thee wed!"

After our brief wedding ceremony and humiliating moments, we had our wedding reception at a service station vending machine that grudgingly produced four Cokes for our wedding party; Sally's sister, Betty, and her husband, Lonnie Baker. Afterward, they dropped us off at a seven dollar a night hotel for a couple of honeymoon hours.

It was a date to remember, February 15, 1951, and we were in love. I was up and gone at 4:00 a.m. for my 6:00 a.m. roll call. What a day and very few hours at night, but we made it. Being financially embarrassed, we couldn't even rent a small room. Betty offered to share their one room apartment and we accepted her offer without hesitating. The close quarter arrangement was made by hanging an army blanket on a clothesline separating the one room. When it was time for bed, the animals at the local zoo had more privacy than the four of us.

Two weeks later, I completed the radar training course and was transferred to Selfridge Air Force Base for reassignment to another base in the Air Defense Command. Sally went back home to her parents in Prescott, Arkansas until I was permanently assigned. Later I read in the newspapers that the Kefauver Committee, headed by Senator Estes Kefauver, was having congressional hearings and investigating lawless activities in Biloxi and the whole state of Mississippi. Soon after the hearings, open gambling and the illegal sale of hard liquor was curtailed.

I was finally assigned to a Radar Aircraft Early Warning Station located near the small farming community of Rockville, Indiana. While I was getting settled at my new duty station, I found a small apartment off base and sent for Sally. With just the two of us, we could begin to live the joys of married life. These included the births of our two daughters. Vicki Lee was born on March 13, 1952 and Michelle Ann was born on January 14, 1954; two beautiful, perfect girls blessed by God and placed in our loving care.

Even though my name had been placed several different times on shipping orders to Korea, it was taken off for one reason or another. We remained at Rockville forty-four months, completing my four year enlistment.

During my tour with the air force, even though I was sent to Radar Operator's School, I never became an operator. I became the unit supply sergeant of the 782nd Aircraft Control and Warning Station, attaining the rank of staff sergeant. On December 1954 my enlistment was up and I was honorably discharged.

With a growing family, we decided to go out into the world of civilians and strive for a better future for our children. After considering our options, we decided to go to Dallas to start a new career. Dallas was a growing city with unlimited opportunities and possibilities. We had obligations and responsibilities to meet, and job stability was a must. In January of 1955, because of my military background, I decided to apply to the City of Dallas for a position as police officer.

There were many favorable factors to be considered: it was more job security, a good retirement plan, and a position of authority and respectability. After a thorough background check, I was finally hired on March 3, 1955.

During the time my application was being processed, Sally had moments filled with anxiety. Before I was accepted as a police officer, preliminary investigations of my personal history were conducted. A police investigator went to the offices where Sally was employed. He asked her how she felt about me becoming a police officer. She indicated she did not particularly want me to do that type of work because of the dangers involved. But, if that was what I wanted as a profession, she would do all she could to help me. The investigator also explained that police work required irregular hours and that I would be away from home many nights.

As the investigator questioned her, many times she wanted to object. But, she was convinced that if a man is content in his work, he is a better husband and father, and is more efficient in his job. After completing the police academy training, I was assigned to the Radio Patrol Division, working with a different officer each night. This was to broaden my police training.

I will never forget my first arrest and traffic citation I issued. My partner instructed me as to the initial approach to the violator and to the procedure in writing the ticket. We had been clocking a man who was speeding in the early morning rush hour traffic. Accelerating up to his vehicle, we flashed our emergency lights and pulled him over to the curb. I was more nervous than the person we stopped. With my hands shaking and my lips quivering, the brief contact with the speedster seemed an eternity. He admitted his guilt and apologized as he drove away. I knew a police officer never forgot his first arrest, but after the first, all the others seemed routine. But was any arrest routine?

In August 1963, my family and I were taking a vacation by automobile to Vinalhaven, Maine to visit my mother. We made our road plans to include a tour of Washington, D.C. and the White House. My children were old enough now to enjoy and absorb the historical significance of our nation's capitol. They would be able to walk where great men of our country and presidents had walked and see the magnificent monuments honoring them.

We lined up with the other tourists to tour the White House, hoping to get a glimpse of President Kennedy or Jackie. We walked slowly through the black iron gates, past the guardhouse and the smartly dressed, crisp-uniformed guards, and stepped inside the door of the White House. In my fantasy, I could almost hear the echoes of closely guarded conversations of the President walking with great leaders of other nations.

Looking up, I saw the wonderful, full-length portrait of President John Fitzgerald Kennedy, standing tall with his head lowered as if deep in thought. Our tour guide pointed out that Mrs. Kennedy had chosen this particular portrait of the President to hang in a prominent place in the White House.

When I voted for President Kennedy in 1960, I never dreamt that someday I would walk in the same hallways and stately rooms of the great and the powerful.

6

CLOSE CALLS

IN JANUARY 1958, due to an unusual number of armed robberies reported, I was assigned to work plainclothes in the Homicide and Robbery Bureau. The division was shorthanded and I was part of a group of patrolmen sent to beef up the unit for a couple of months. My duties were to team up with a seasoned detective and would involve investigating armed robberies, homicides, and reported rapes.

There had been a string of armed robberies of motels, service stations, and convenience stores, and it was determined that one person using the same M.O. was the perpetrator. His method was to make the clerks take off their pants, and he would tie knots in them and toss them outside. He would force them to a back room or into a refrigerated cooler. The news media tagged him the "pants bandit."

Analyzing his selection of previous targets, we began a series of stakeouts at area motels and convenience stores in an effort to anticipate his next robbery. A random pattern developed; he never hit the same place twice or anywhere near his last robbery. But, we were going to out-smart him and be ready for him on his next try. So we thought! He was finally caught except not by the police. He attempted to rob a service station, but the attendant wrestled the gun from him. during the struggle the gun went off and the bullet struck the robber in his foot. The attendant finally gained possession of the pistol. When he saw the robber was wounded he actually returned the pistol to him. The robber seized the opportunity and promptly shot the attendant.

The service station attendant was sent to the hospital and was lying on a gurney waiting to be treated. To his amazement, when he looked at the gurney next to him there was the robber waiting for treatment of his wound. The service station attendant starting yelling to a hospital security officer, "That's the son-of-a-bitch that shot me!"

The security officer promptly detained the gunman and held him for the police. This unlikely event resulted in clearing over fifty robberies off the books. He copped a plea and received fifty-six years in the Texas State Penitentiary.

IN ANOTHER INCIDENT, we were cruising the streets in the general vicinity where an armed robbery had been reported involving four neighborhood taverns. With my partner, Walter Potts, we started combing the neighborhood bars searching for the suspect described over the police radio. We were in a nearby bar that had not yet been hit and spotted a man matching the description of the suspect. We eyeballed the redheaded guy that sat on the barstool at the counter. When he reached for his glass of beer, his jacket raised with his arm and I could see a pistol tucked in his belt. Detective Potts whispered to me, "Go for his pistol and at the same time I'll knock him off his barstool."

I nodded in agreement and we headed toward him. Brushing by him, I jerked the pistol from his waist. My partner knocked him from his perch down to the floor and cuffed him. The robber had instructed his victims to place all the money in a plain, brown paper bag. There on the counter was a paper bag where he had been sitting. I recovered the money from the four robberies. The pistol he carried was a fully loaded .32 automatic.

When it was time to testify at his trial his lawyer tried to throw in a "dead ringer." Unknown to me this guy had an identical, red haired, twin brother. The defense lawyer brought in the twins and had them sitting next to each other at the defense table. Due to my training in keen observation, I remembered that the man we arrested in the robberies parted his red hair on the left. Just by pure chance the identical twin parted his on the right. I was able to identify the true robber and he was found guilty.

On the rare occasions when I related my experiences and close calls to Sally, she realized the dangers I was confronted with in my daily duties. It was something she had to cope with each time I left for work. I know she often wondered if I would return to her and the girls alive.

AFTER NINETY DAYS, I returned to uniformed patrol duties. It was May 25, 1959 and I was a one-man squad. I heard the disturbance call to Squad 91 and I started driving in the general direction of the call. A couple of minutes later, the dispatcher advised Squad 91 that the disturbance was now reported to be a shooting. Since I was near the location, I decided to answer the call as backup. I arrived about the same time as Officers Behringer and Anglin who made up Squad 91.

When we walked to the front door, I noticed water was hastily used to wash away blood although it was still visible on the walk leading to the porch. When we got inside the screen porch, I noticed a pile of rags and papers. My curiosity got the better of me. I lifted the papers and there was a man lying lifeless with a bullet hole in his forehead. He was dressed in painter's striped overalls. His eyes were glazed and stared straight up at me.

There was no response when we knocked on the front door. We heard scuffling noises and mumbling behind the door. We continued to bang on the door, announcing that we were the police and to open up. Still no response. Turning around, we saw our supervisor, Sergeant P.T. Dean, driving up. I advised him on the situation. I asked his permission to kick down the door. Sergeant Dean replied, "Go ahead and kick it down!" I started toward the door and was about to kick it in when Sergeant Dean said, "Wait a minute, Nick. Maybe we had better wait until we get some more help out here." This reevaluation probably saved my life!

We later learned that the man who shot and killed the workman I found dead on the porch was standing behind the front door, and was going to shoot the first officer who came through. I realized that I would have been that officer.

The help we requested arrived a short time later. We surrounded the house and used portable speakers, trying to coax the gunman out and to surrender his weapons and hostages. He had taken six hostages, threatening to kill all of them. To prevent their escape, he chained them together. Ignoring our demands, he fired several gunshots from the window as we took cover behind the trees. A barrage of tear-gas was fired into an open window. The hostages, overcome by the gas, started crawling from the window, still chained together. They were coughing and gasping for air. Ducking as low as I could, I rushed to their aid. I helped them clear the tiny window and led them to safety. We tried to learn from the hostages the exact location of the man in the house. They couldn't tell us because the thick teargas smoke had blanketed their view of him and, in turn, aided in their escape.

I returned to the tree I had used as cover and started firing into the open window used for their escape. Other officers started firing, but the order was given to cease fire. The house was going to be sprayed by a machine gun. I was summoned by a senior officer to cover the rear of the house. I laid in the grass and kept my head to the ground while the interior of the house was sprayed by machine gun fire. If the gunman tried to escape from the back of the house, I was to stop him. As they sprayed the house, I heard and felt the movement of bullets whizzing near my head. With each blast of gunfire, I buried myself deeper in the weeds and tall grass.

Someone shouted it was over. Dusting myself off, I went to the front and the officers were carrying the gunman, Frank Winsor, out of the bullet riddled house. He was lying dead on a stretcher waiting for his journey to the morgue. It had been a long, anxious, and frightening two hours.

Frank Winsor's actions were detailed to us by his hostages. The night before, Frank Winsor came by his landlady's house and took her hostage. He needed more hostages so he forced her to call her neighbors and make up a reason for them to come to her house.

As they arrived, Winsor chained them up one-by-one, and told them he would kill them all if they didn't do as they were told. Keeping them chained together throughout the night, he constantly threatened bodily harm.

The sheriff had evicted Frank Winsor and his wife from their apartment for being past due on the rent. When they were forced to move, he was convinced the sheriff was to blame for the death of his wife's pet canary, which he felt caused the death of his wife. He was irrational and his plan was to trade the hostages for the sheriff, and in turn trade the sheriff for the governor.

Frank Winsor killed the man on the porch because he came to the landlady's house for a set of keys to a rental house he had been contracted to paint. When Winsor pointed his gun at him, the painter panicked and started to run. Winsor shot him in cold blood. He forced the hostages to drag the body back on the porch and hide him. They were ordered to scrub the blood from the walkway in an attempt to delay discovery of the crime.

When Winsor saw the police approaching, he told the hostages he couldn't handle the police, and if they cried out or made a sound, he would kill them all. He stated before he would be arrested, the police would have to kill him. After spraying the house with gunfire, the officers rushed the house and found Frank Winsor had committed suicide by shooting himself in the head.

IT WAS LATE in the afternoon of a very hot August day and a call over the radio came regarding an attempted suicide. I wasn't far from the address and arrived at the scene before the ambulance. As I was getting out of my squad car, I could hear the screams of a woman and a man's voice yelling and swearing. Rushing through the open screen door, I saw a woman sitting astride a man who was on his back on the bed. The man had grasped a hunting knife in his right hand and was attempting to cut his own throat. The woman was trying desperately to prevent her husband from cutting his own throat, but his strength was no match for her. The bed sheets were splattered with his blood. He had inflicted several cuts to his neck and was bleeding profusely.

My first thought was to gain control of his knife. We struggled and suddenly the blade broke. He was left without a weapon to end his desire to live. Breaking down, he cried, "Why wouldn't you let me die?"

When the ambulance finally arrived the paramedics attended to his wounds and took him to the hospital. His wife said her husband had been very ill, and he was convinced he would never be well again. Recently he was discharged from the V.A. hospital where they told him there was nothing else that could be done. They also told him that his sickness was all his head, referring him to outpatient psychoanalysis. Losing faith in the V.A. doctors, he made the decision to take his own life.

IN YET ANOTHER knife wielding incident, we received a call from a nursing home late at night. When we arrived, the night duty nurse met us at the front porch. In a calm but guarded voice she said, "One of the patients is threatening everyone with a knife and daring them to enter his room. He won't let us give him his medication."

As quietly as we could, we climbed the creaky stairs. The old house had been converted to a nursing home. Reaching the second floor, I could see a pitiful looking old gentleman standing in the doorway of his room. In his right hand he firmly held a small paring knife, daring us to come any closer. I explained we were police officers and we were there to help him. He stated unequivocally, "I don't care who you are, you are not coming into my room! These nurses are trying to poison me with their medicine. I am not going to take it." Realizing his senility contributed to his unreasonableness, I started talking to him as if I were talking to a child. I inched up closer trying to get within arms-length. Engaging in meaningless conversation, I tried to divert his attention from his knife. I was throwing questions one after the other before he could answer completely to confuse him even more.

He was beginning to get nervous and I noticed he began to change the knife to the other hand to scratch himself. This action would give me an opportunity to knock it out of his hand. Sure enough, he changed hands again and I knocked the knife to the floor. Picking it up, I smiled confident that I solved the problem. The old gentleman went over to his bed, lifted the mattress and pulled out an even larger knife.

I thought, *How can I get this butcher knife away from him this time? Do I dare try the same trick?* It wasn't very long before he changed hands again. Staring into his eyes, I calmly reached over and grabbed the knife. Wanting to make sure he was out of weapons, I searched his bed and the entire room, collecting an arsenal of cutting tools. There was everything from razor blades to beer can openers. I told him to behave himself and that the nurses were there to help not to harm him. He retreated to his bed like a scolded, punished child.

I felt sorry for this old gentleman who once lived a full and useful life. The nurse said his family never visited and he felt forgotten. I was sure the attention he received, even though it was negative, helped to alleviate some of those feelings.

THERE WAS ANOTHER close call but not for me. While cruising my patrol district, I received a call to meet an ambulance regarding an injured person. Fortunately, I was a short distance from the address. The mother of a small baby came rushing to the street to meet me, cradling her baby in her arms. The mother was crying and screaming hysterically that her boy wasn't breathing. I took the child from her extended arms and placed the little boy on the grass. I could tell the baby wasn't breathing.

I remembered reading a recent article in *Reader's Digest* illustrating a technique of mouth-to-mouth resuscitation. We had never been given this procedure in our police training. Without hesitation, I started the resuscitation. His little face had turned a pale blue and I couldn't see any signs of life in his small body. I continued to force my breath into his lungs and carefully placed my hand on his chest, pressing gently but firmly, forcing my breath from his lungs. A small glimmer of life returned and he began to sob, trying to breathe on his own.

Suddenly, he stopped breathing and it appeared something was still lodged in his windpipe. I gathered him up and rushed in the house and stretched him out on a couch. Once again I started the procedure, forcing more of my breath into his mouth. I worked frantically trying to revive him. He began taking short breaths again and this time he coughed up his breakfast. He began crying and screaming as he gasped for air. My face was splashed with his vomit, but that didn't matter. He was breathing again.

At that moment the ambulance arrived. The paramedics put the little boy in the ambulance and immediately placed the resuscitator over his face. With the mother at her baby's side the ambulance howled away with sirens and lights flashing, speeding to the hospital.

I stayed with the father to get the necessary information for my required reports.

I asked how it happened and he replied, "While we were eating breakfast, the baby started choking on his food and suddenly stopped breathing. I guess we panicked and didn't know what to do except call for help." He thanked me for taking control of a life and death situation and saving the life of his little boy. Without speaking his face expressed all the gratitude I would ever need.

I went directly to the hospital to make a "follow up" on the child. In the emergency room, I met the doctor who said he would not have survived without my help. The doctor explained I had cleared the obstruction.

I left the hospital with a wonderful glow inside, realizing I had saved a human life. Reading that article and putting it to a real life-saving test was the most rewarding personal experience in my whole career as a police officer.

ONE HOT, HUMID afternoon near the end of my duty while taking a short break from the August heat, I seized the opportunity to catch up on my accumulated paperwork on minor police incident reports. I was languishing leisurely in one of our most southern fire stations waiting to use the telephone to call in my reports to a police clerk. A couple of the firemen were polishing the fire engine. Four other firemen were in a slamming domino game, enjoying the comfort of their air conditioned firehouse.

As I glanced their way, they shouted in unison as if rehearsed, "Hey, officer, how's the weather out there?"

With a frown and sweat dripping from my chin, I said, "Man, you guys got it made in the shade!"

I knew that I wouldn't trade jobs with them for anything. They may seem to be busy doing nothing or making little chores like cleaning equipment to pass time, but I knew when they were putting out death dealing, intense fires they were performing one of the most dangerous occupations. It's unimaginable what they go through, running inside burning buildings and homes, attempting to save human or even animal life. They have no regard for their own safety.

Suddenly, a woman ran inside the fire station in a panic.

"Mr. Fireman, please hurry. There's a snake behind my couch in the living room!"

"Lady, you see the police officer over there lounging by the telephone. Go tell him. If that snake has caused a fire, we'll go. Otherwise, we don't fool with snakes."

I said, "Hey, you guys rescue cats out of trees don't you?"

"Yeah, but that's another story."

Secretly, I have a real phobia about snakes of any kind. I got up immediately and gently took the lady by the arm and said, "Let's go get that bad ol' snake." I placed her in my squad car and drove the short distance to her house.

"Where exactly is that snake?"

"The last time I saw it, it was behind my couch!"

Walking slowly into the living room to the couch, I saw the snake crawling into the kitchen. It was a long, brown snake. It slithered behind the refrigerator and quickly disappeared behind the kitchen cabinets. I asked the lady if she had any garden tools I could use.

She went into the attached garage and returned with a hoe. It had a small blade on one side and on the other was a two-pronged digging fork. Taking the hoe from her, I eased the prongs in the cabinet door handles and slowly opened the doors. I saw the snake curled around the pipes. Using the prongs, I attempted to place them around the body of the snake, but it crawled out of sight behind the silverware drawers. I hooked the prongs in the drawer handle and gently pulled it open. The snake was coiled in the back of the drawer. Again using the prongs, I managed to slip the fork underneath his body. I pulled on the hoe handle and the snake began wrapping his body around the prongs.

"I've got you now, you slippery devil!"

In attempting to dislodge it from the drawer, I made a desperate pull on the hoe handle. To my surprise, I pulled the snake out with mild resistance. The force I used to lift the hoe sent the snake flying to the ceiling. The snake suddenly dropped from the prongs and fell at my feet with its mouth open, ready to strike. I quickly turned the blade and started chopping at the snake. Striking the snake, I cut it into several pieces and smashed its head. I gathered the mutilated snake body and took the pieces out to the backyard and hung them on the fence. Looking at the remnants of the snake, I discovered the snake was a poisonous copperhead.

When I returned to the kitchen, I found that I had chopped and damaged the lady's linoleum in the process of killing it. I got the job done even though my adrenaline had reached a new high.

I apologized for cutting up her floor, but she said, "Oh, don't worry about it. I was going to get new linoleum for the kitchen anyway." She thanked me and I left smiling. I felt satisfied that I had eased the lady's mind, removing her present danger, without delay.

I could have called Animal Control and they would have removed the reptile except the danger to this lady was now and very real to her. She wanted immediate action.

The Animal Control personnel would have taken hours to get there and the snake would have been more difficult to find the longer we waited. I drove away feeling good about myself and the whole situation. Now, I was ready to go about my real police work.

7

THE PRESIDENTIAL PARTY ARRIVES

THE PERSISTENT BUZZING of the clock radio awakened us from the early morning hours of deep and peaceful sleep. My wife, Sally, was up and about immediately, making coffee and beginning the morning rituals. In my somnolence, I could hear the light rain as it dripped from the roof. Secretly, I was wishing I could just lie in my warm bed and listen to the soft music of light rain, rhythmically returning me to my dreams. But duty called and I had to submit to reality.

During my shower, I realized it was the day that President Kennedy, with his entourage, would visit our city. I thought to myself, *I hope it stops raining so there will be more people out on the streets to see him.* I hoped everything would go smoothly and without incident. I felt confident everything would be all right and that our boys would be capable of handling any situation. Everyone involved in his protection had been assigned to their individual duties.

The sergeant reassigned a couple of extra men to Love Field to help with the arrival of the Presidential party. The rest of us were to go about our regular police duties. J.D. Tippit, like the majority of the men working those daytime hours, was to be a one-man squad and assigned to his regular District 78. His area of responsibility was located in the southernmost part of the city, residential, with light businesses intermingled.

My district was more congested and more populated, but the area of patrol was much smaller. I was a senior training officer and one of my responsibilities was to instruct and train new police officers that had just graduated from the police academy. My rookie partner, T.R. Gregory, was in his third month of training and was going to be an exceptional officer.

Outwardly, I expressed how glad I was not to disrupt my regular duties by being involved in the President's visit. In my mind though, I secretly wanted to be a part of his protection. Perhaps, just perhaps, I'd get a glimpse or even get a chance to shake his or Jackie's hand.

It was still drizzling rain as I drove to my reporting duty station, the Oak Cliff police substation. The dreariness of the clouds and falling rain were discouraging. In the locker room as I changing into my uniform, I exchanged trivial conversation with J.D. Tippit. We were lockermates and always kidded each other to lighten up and ease the stress that came with the job. He was very likeable and good-natured, able to take a joke, as well as hand one out. He was liked by all of the men he worked with and very conscientious in his police duties. One could always rely on J.D. Tippit in any situation.

I remember two occasions when death had stalked J.D. He and his partner answered a domestic disturbance call to a residence in West Dallas, the city's housing projects. As they knocked on the door, a hysterical woman opened it and invited them inside. Her irate, drunken husband was crouching behind the opened door. When they entered, he struck out with a rusty ice pick, stabbing one officer in the knee and stabbing J.D. in the shoulder. With their wounds they were still able to subdue and arrest the attacker. Both officers recovered without serious injuries.

The other incident was more threatening. Tippit and his partner, Dale Hankins, were called to a tavern on a disturbance with a gun. As they faced a crazed drunk, he raised a .45 pistol and pulled the trigger point blank at J.D.'s head. Both officers pulled their pistols and shot the man dead on the spot. When the .45 was examined, it was found that the attacker had loaded it with the wrong caliber ammunition.

At 7:30 a.m. I reported for duty along with the other officers of my platoon. I answered to morning roll call and detail. We never expected or suspected the coming tragedies. The light rain stopped at approximately 8:30 a.m. The clouds disappeared and the sun was brightly shining upon our city, drying the streets rapidly. I thought maybe this welcome change in the weather would aid the motorists to be accident free on their way to work. It was going to be a beautiful day after all. Hopefully, many would turn out to welcome President John Kennedy and Jackie to show their enthusiasm, and give the Presidential party respect and support.

All morning my partner and I had been cruising around our patrol district attending to the normal duties and functions of a regular police unit, answering the needs of our citizens. We were well aware of the President's visit but were so removed from the places he would appear I didn't dwell on it. I tried to be unconcerned and disassociated. Deep inside I felt uneasy, tense and apprehensive. I knew I would feel this way until they had all departed to San Antonio, Texas, which was their next stop.

Several days before President Kennedy and his party were to visit Dallas, we were briefed as to how to control situations should any arise. We were primarily concerned with extreme right groups or any individuals who might exhibit disrespect to the President. We wanted to avoid similar incidents that had occurred during the visit of Lyndon B. Johnson and Adlai Stevenson. I had high hopes and felt the President was being accepted in a great and dignified manner. We had reports of a large and happy crowd at Love Field greeting the President and his party as well as reports of large crowds along the motorcade route.

Around noon we pulled in front of a favorite cafeteria for lunch, checking out of service with the dispatcher. We almost completed the meal when the cashier came to our table and said excitedly, "President Kennedy has been shot!"

I said, "You must be kidding?"

"No," she replied. "I just heard it on my radio!"

As I looked into her eyes, her expression revealed doubt and her statement was more of a question than a fact. Even as she spoke the words, she didn't appear to believe what she had said. I turned, reached for my police cap, and hurriedly said, "Let's get out of here and get on the police radio and check it out!"

We rushed out of the cafeteria, and by this time it was 12:30 p.m. As we listened closely, the alert signal of the police radio was heard throughout the city: "All available police units report code three to the triple underpass, Elm and Houston. There has been a shooting in the presidential motorcade! No other information available at this time!"

I gave my call number to the police dispatcher, "95 is en route, code three!" and activated the emergency lights and siren. I kept thinking, *Oh God! No! We must hurry! I cannot believe this. It can't be happening! Please, dear God, let it be a mistake. Don't let anything happen to the President or his party!* A million questions raced through my mind. How? Why? And most important…*who?*

I prayed to God that it wasn't the President.

8

MOOD OF DALLAS

THE MOOD OF the people of Dallas prior to the planned visit of President Kennedy was a mixture of pros and cons. The President's intention to pay a visit to Texas in the fall of 1963 aroused interest throughout the state. The two Dallas newspapers provided their readers with a steady stream of information and speculation about the trip, beginning on September 13. The *Dallas Times-Herald* announced in the front page article that President Kennedy was planning a brief one-day tour of four Texas cities—Dallas, Fort Worth, San Antonio, and Houston. Both Dallas papers cited White House sources on September 26, confirming the President's intention to visit Texas on November 21 and 22, with Dallas scheduled as one of the stops.

Articles, editorials, and letters to the editor in *The Dallas Morning News* and the *Dallas Times-Herald*, after September 13, reflected the feeling in the community about the forthcoming Presidential visit. Although there were critical editorials and letters to the editors, the news stories reflected the desire of Dallas officials to welcome the President with dignity and courtesy. An editorial in the *Dallas Times-Herald* of September 17 called on the people of Dallas to be "congenial hosts" even though "Dallas didn't vote for Mr. Kennedy in 1960, may not endorse him in '64."

On October 3, *The Dallas Morning News* quoted U.S. Representative Joe Pool's hope that President Kennedy would receive a "good welcome" and would not face demonstrations like those encountered by Vice President Johnson during the 1960 campaign.[8]

President Kennedy's visit to Texas in November 1963 had been under consideration for almost a year before it occurred. He had made only a few brief visits to the state since the 1960 Presidential campaign, and in 1962 he began to consider a formal visit. During 1963 the reasons for making the trip became more persuasive. As a political leader, the President wished to resolve the factional controversy within the Democratic Party in Texas before the election of 1964. The party itself saw an opportunity to raise funds by having the President speak at a political dinner eventually planned in Austin. As Chief of State, the President always welcomed the opportunity to learn, firsthand, about the problems which concerned the American people. Moreover, he looked forward to the public appearances that he personally enjoyed.[9]

Increased concern about the President's visit was aroused by the incident involving the U.S. Ambassador to the United Nations, Adlai E. Stevenson. On the evening of October 24, 1963 after addressing a meeting in Dallas, Stevenson was jeered, jostled, and spat upon by hostile demonstrators outside the Dallas Memorial Auditorium Theater. The local, national, and international reaction to this incident evoked from Dallas officials and newspapers strong condemnations of the demonstrators. Mayor Earle Cabell called on the city to redeem itself during President Kennedy's visit. He asserted that Dallas had shed its reputation of the 1920s as the "Southwest hate capital of Dixie."

On October 26, the press reported Chief of Police Curry's plans to call in one hundred extra off-duty officers to help protect President Kennedy. Any thought that the President might cancel his visit to Dallas was ended when Governor Connally confirmed on November 8 that the President would come to Texas on November 21-22, and that he would visit San Antonio, Houston, Fort Worth, Dallas, and Austin.[10]

During November the Dallas papers frequently reported plans for protecting the President, stressing the thoroughness of the preparations. They conveyed the pleas of Dallas leaders that citizens not demonstrate or create disturbances during the President's visit. On November 18, the Dallas City Council adopted a new city ordinance prohibiting interference with attendance at lawful assemblies. Two days before the President's arrival Chief Curry warned that the Dallas police would not permit improper conduct during his visit.

Meanwhile on November 17, the president of the Dallas Chamber of Commerce referred to the city's reputation of being the friendliest town in America and asserted that citizens would "greet the President of the United States with the warmth and pride that keep the Dallas spirit famous the world over." Two days later, a local Republican leader called for a "civilized nonpartisan" welcome for President Kennedy, stating that "in many respects Dallas County has isolated itself from the main stream of life in the world in this decade."

Another hostile reaction to the impending visit came to a head shortly before his arrival. On November 21 there appeared on the streets of Dallas the anonymous handbill. It was fashioned after the "wanted" circulars issued by law enforcement agencies. Beneath two photographs of President Kennedy, one full face and one profile, appeared the caption "Wanted for Treason," followed by a scurrilous bill of particulars vilifying the President. On the morning of the President's arrival, there appeared in *The Dallas Morning News* a full page, black-bordered advertisement headed "Welcome Mr. Kennedy to Dallas." It was sponsored by The American Fact-Finding Committee, which the sponsor later testified was an ad hoc committee "formed strictly for the purpose of having a name to put in the paper." The "welcome" consisted of a series of statements and questions critical of the President and his administration.[11]

Along with the physical security arrangements requested by the Secret Service for the airport, motorcade, and Trade Mart luncheon, Dallas Police were attempting to keep known members of certain groups under surveillance. Some of the more active groups in Dallas at the time were:

>The Ku [sic] Klux Klan
>Indignant White Citizens [sic] Council
>National States Rights Party
>John Birch Society
>Dallas White Citizens [sic] Council
>Oak Cliff White Citizens [sic] Council
>The General Edwin A. Walker Group
>American Opinion Forum
>Dallas Committee for Full Citizenship
>Young Peoples [sic] Socialist League
>Dallas Civil Liberties Union
>Texas White Citizens [sic] Council
>Black Muslims

Previous to the President's visit it was determined that only two of these organizations were planning demonstrations during the President's visit to Dallas. The General Edwin A. Walker Group intended to picket the parade route and the

Trade Mart, and the Indignant White Citizens [sic] Council was preparing signs to picket the Trade Mart.

9

THE SHOOTINGS

WE FINALLY ARRIVED. Ten long, frightful minutes had elapsed since the terrible explosions of the first shots. Hundreds of people had gathered at the scene of this tragedy. Police were everywhere. Dealey Plaza and the grassy knoll abounded with spectators and police officers, all with drawn faces. Uniformed and plainclothes officers were on the railroad tracks above the triple underpass, detaining and questioning suspects. They had entered and closed off the Texas School Book Depository.

    I maneuvered my squad car through the immense crowd and the gridlocked traffic to a point on Elm Street. I stopped in the traffic lane as near as possible to the curb. We left our police car just above the fatal curve that led into the triple underpass. People were craning their necks and pointing to the windows high above in the red brick building. The Hertz Rent-A-Car sign was flashing the current temperature and time...12:41. I also noticed officers in uniforms and plainclothes ushering individuals from the crowd and leading them away. I wondered to myself if they were participants in the shootings or mere witnesses. I didn't see any confiscated weapons.

We reported to the nearest supervisor. He instructed us to help gain control of the milling crowd. He said, "Push them back around the corner and rope it off and keep them behind the ropes. There may be more shots from the building!" My partner and I carried out his orders, and along with other officers backed the wedging crowd out of the street to the protection of the buildings on upper Elm Street. We had set up the first police line and were controlling this area.

With my back to the crowd, I scanned the windows and rooftop of the building, hoping upon hope that I could observe something unusual or suspicious. I was thinking, *What can I do now? Was this all I could do? Just stand in the street and stare at the crowd, and watch scores of police officers go into that red brick building?*

The building was plainly identified with Texas School Book Depository above the door. It was completely surrounded. The railroad yards and standing boxcars were being searched. Police officers were everywhere with their shotguns in readiness. I felt I needed to do something to help, but what? There were police vehicles of all types in the street with their radios blaring continuing conversations, and giving updated reports and information on all suspicious actions being reported from all over the city.

Then the police dispatcher transmitted the terrible news, "The President was pronounced dead at 1:00 p.m. at Parkland Hospital. Governor Connally is in critical condition. Time, 1:16 p.m."

As I lowered my head in silent grief, the tears welled in my eyes. Suddenly, a voice—a loud, uncontrolled voice—unfamiliar to police radio procedure began shouting over the police radio waves. "A policeman has just been shot! He is lying in the street and looks like he is dead. I am a citizen using his radio."

Police dispatcher, "Where are you?"

"We are at Tenth and Patton. This is car number 10!"

I was stunned, dumbfounded, and shocked. I felt the blood drain from my body and a cold chill ran up my spine. I knew that J.D. Tippit was driving car number 10. I went to the supervisor and asked if we could go to Oak Cliff and help find the suspect that shot Tippit. He gave us permission to leave. I knew that most of the officers would be more concentrated at the scene of the assassination and Parkland Hospital where they had taken President Kennedy and Governor Connally.

We ran to our squad car and started racing to yet another tragedy. A fellow officer and a good friend had been felled by an unknown assailant as the President had. Why? Who? Tragic events were occurring too fast. I didn't have time to grieve openly. My mind was racing with anxiety. My heart was fiercely pounding with every breath. I could see my badge moving with every beat of my heart. En-route we heard the police dispatcher in a monotone of grief announce, "Officer J.D. Tippit was pronounced D.O.A. at Methodist Hospital." He was shot and murdered just three short miles from the assassination site.

I thought to myself, *This murderer must be stopped. Somehow, someway, he must not get away. I must compose myself and reconstruct my thoughts.* Being familiar with the area of the most recent shooting, I was hoping to be more productive in this renewed manhunt. I tried to visualize what the perpetrator would do. I knew he must be running in fear after killing a cop. Running between houses, darting through alleyways—or maybe he was trying to conceal himself in hedgerows—or lying in wait in a house or building. Or, he could be calmly walking down the street, mingling with curious and excited crowds.

A description was relayed, "To all police units. Be on the lookout for a white male, in his twenties, five feet six inches, one hundred-sixty pounds, wearing a light colored jacket or shirt, dark trousers, slender build, armed with a pistol. Last seen running south from Tenth and Patton."

There would be no reason to go directly to the scene of the shooting, so I was anxiously trying to head off the suspect. I took the Jefferson Boulevard exit from R.L. Thornton Freeway and approached south of the scene of the Tippit shooting.

If we are lucky, I thought, *we may see him fleeing down one of the streets.*

Approaching the 400 block of East Jefferson Boulevard, I was waved down by Sergeant G.L. Hill who took charge of my partner. He needed another man to search a house where a suspect was reported to be hiding. That was the last I saw of my rookie partner until later that afternoon. I continued patrolling alone, cruising the streets and alleyways.

I checked every report fruitlessly. A report came out that a suspicious person was seen running into the public library at Marsalis and Jefferson just two blocks from the shooting of Officer Tippit. I was only a block away. I rushed to the library and stopped my squad car in the alley west of the library, and bailed out with shotgun in hand. Approaching the basement entrance, I ordered everyone out with their hands up. I jacked a round into the chamber, a very definite and demanding sound; at ten yards away, it would cut a man in half. I was not taking any unnecessary chances. A frightened boy of sixteen and the employees of the library came out with arms raised above their heads.

With quizzical expressions on their faces, one lady asked, "What's wrong?"

I replied, "I had a report of a suspect that was seen running into the library."

The young boy explained, "I just ran in to tell everyone that President Kennedy had been assassinated." I was satisfied with his explanation and advised them to go back inside.

Let down, but feeling some relief, I returned to my squad car and placed the shotgun back in its rack. Sliding behind the wheel, I heard the police radio reporting that another suspicious person had run into the Texas Theatre and was hiding in the balcony. I was just a few blocks away and I started racing once again.

10

THE ARREST & CAPTURE OF OSWALD

AS I APPROACHED the front of the Texas Theatre, I noticed several police cars were already there. The officers had left their vehicles and entered through the front entrance to the lobby.

I rushed to the alley to the rear of the theatre. There were several officers standing in the alley with their shotguns raised and guarding the exit doors. I decided I would try to enter the ground rear exit door. The door would not open from the outside. I started banging, shaking, and pulling on the heavy metal door. Suddenly, the door opened and two men dressed in civilian suits were inside.

One of the men was Johnny Brewer, whom I later found out was the witness that observed the suspect dart into the theatre. Johnny Brewer deserves much credit for alerting the police and reporting the movements of a suspicious person. Johnny was a manager for a shoe store located down the street from the Texas Theatre. He was in his store when he noticed a man stop inside the foyer of the shop windows and duck his head when a police car sped by. The man hurried to the sidewalk, up the street, and when he got to the theatre he walked in without purchasing a ticket. Johnny observed this irrational behavior and followed him to the theatre.

Johnny asked the ticket clerk, Julia Postal, "Did you see the guy go inside?"

She replied, "No!"

Johnny said, "You had better call the police because this guy is trying to hide from them."

After I had entered the Texas Theatre, I went to the exit curtains to the left of the movie screen. As I peeked through the heavy curtains out into the audience, I could see the suspect whom Johnny Brewer had pointed out to me. He was seated in the rear of the main floor, three rows from the partition of the lobby, second chair from the right center aisle.

As I searched his eyes, he was staring straight ahead watching the movie, unconcerned. Unconcerned of the sudden appearance of many police officers that had entered the theatre searching for a suspect in the shooting of Officer J.D. Tippit. As I was deciding my plan of action, I noticed that there were only ten or fifteen patrons for this Friday matinee showing of the double-billed features, *Cry of Battle* and *War is Hell*. How factual these titles would relate to the reality of the situation in just a few moments.

I made my decision. I thought, *I will try an act of diversion. I will search the two men seated in the middle near the front of the movie screen nearest to me, and then search everyone in turn as I get to them. This indirect approach may cause him to think that I am not considering him. I am not going to take any unnecessary chances by missing anyone or anything, in anyway. One small mistake could cost another life! Maybe mine!*

After searching the first two men and finding nothing, I started walking toward him. Slowly and deliberately, I was closing the distance between us. Maybe, just maybe, I could prevent a standoff and a shootout if I could get close enough.

My pistol remained strapped in my holster. My hand was open and swinging free along my side. My searching eyes were more concentrated on two other persons seated to my left just a few steps from my target. But, I was keeping him in my vision from the corner of my eyes. Detecting no movement or change in his position, I continued walking calmly up the aisle, trying to act as if I were going to pass him by.

This small element of surprise might buy me some time. Like a hunter, I was secretly stalking the prey. I had this strange sensation that everyone in the theatre had their eyes fixed on me and was watching my every move. I was almost there.

Still no movement from him. The diversion was working. I turned suddenly and stepped quickly into his row. Moving closer, I noticed his empty hands were folded in his lap. As he calmly looked up at me, I spoke with a strong voice of authority, "Get on your feet!" He had suddenly realized he had waited too long to make a free and open move of aggression. He stood slowly facing the movie screen. Turning his head to me, we were face-to-face. I stared directly into his eyes. In attempting to conceal his guilt, his expression changed to surprise and innocence like that of a child.

Without a command, he started bringing both hands up and in a voice of resignation, he spoke softly, "Well, it's all over now."

I thought, *He's giving up!* For a moment, I was surprised in the simplicity of the arrest. *I had him now!* My hands started reaching for his waist to make the routine search for a weapon. His left hand had reached eye level and his right hand was raised shoulder high.

Suddenly, his left hand made a tight fist and it exploded between my eyes. *My God, this is it! He's not giving up after all!* The unexpected blow knocked my head back and my police cap flew from my head and momentarily rocked my balance.

With the same darting movement, his right hand went to his waist. With my left hand, I could feel him pulling a pistol from under his shirt. An automatic reaction of aggression began physically before my brain could command me. He was bringing the pistol up to my chest. I grabbed for it with my left hand, and grasped the pistol firmly over the cylinder and the hammer with all the strength I could muster. I felt the hammer glide under my hand as he pulled the trigger. The returning hammer made a dull, audible snapping sound, as the firing pin struck the flesh of my hand, between the thumb and forefinger. Bracing myself, I stood rigid, waiting for the bullet to penetrate my chest. Somehow, the miracle of my strength impeded the action of the cylinder and the hammer.

The bullet beneath the firing pin did not receive the full striking force and slightly dented the primer of the shell. Pivoting his pistol to the side and away from my body, I realized I was not shot. With a clutched fist I hit him over his left eye, knocking him into the seat. With a lunge of desperation, I fell on top of him and my body completely covered his. I was trying to smother his movements. I was desperately struggling for possession of his pistol. I knew that he couldn't hurt me with his fists; I also knew that I could be seriously wounded or killed with his pistol. Our arms and elbows were entangled with our twisting and turning bodies. My life depended on gaining complete control of his weapon. I managed to grasp the handle of his pistol with my right hand and jerked it away from him.

I pushed the muzzle in his stomach for a fleeting moment. He tried to kill me and I'd be justified in killing him! But I had second thoughts. There was no need to shoot him now that I had control of his weapon. I was also afraid that if I did shoot him the bullet might go through him, through the back of the seat and hit one of the officers who had come to my aid.

I pulled the pistol away and handed it to one of the officers standing in the aisle.

I called out to my fellow officers around me, "I've got him!" We handcuffed him, and the officers that came to my aid took my prisoner away from me and led him out of the theatre. On their way out, I heard him using obscenities and making accusations of police brutality. He was saying, "That policeman hit me! Don't hit me anymore! Why am I being arrested? I haven't done anything!"

For a few moments I sat down in one of the seats trying to catch my breath and regain my strength and composure, and going over in my mind what had just occurred; all that had happened was within a span of a few moments. I felt empty and abandoned. I was left alone in the silent, darkened theatre. The adrenaline had subsided with another close one.

11

I GOT HIM, SARGE!

I FOUND MY police cap several rows down from the scene of the struggle. Dusting it off, I placed in on my head and I walked out the front of the theatre. Outside, I was met by my fellow officer and close friend, Frank Williams. He took out a handkerchief and wiped the blood, sweat, and tears from my face. I could see the sadness and deep concern in his face that only a good friend could express with simple kindness.

Frank said, "Are you alright?"

I answered with a fabricated smile. "Yes, I'm okay."

It was just what I needed. It made me feel good that someone was concerned about me at this trying time. I noticed a large crowd had gathered on the sidewalk and I asked Frank, "What have they done with my prisoner?"

"The crowd was getting out of hand and they were shouting, 'kill the son-of-a-bitch, he killed the President!' so the officers put him in a car and took him to City Hall."

A photographer outside the theatre had already photographed the other officers taking the suspect out and I was not with them because I had to retrieve my police hat. As it happened my prisoner, the most wanted man in America, and I the arresting officer, were never photographed together.

Captain Westbrook walked up to me and looked at my face and said, "How badly are you hurt, son?"

I replied, "Oh, I'm okay. Just a few scratches and bruises."

He looked closer at my face and said, "Report to headquarters and let's get your face photographed at the crime lab. We might need photographic evidence that he resisted arrest and caused injury to you. As you may or may not know, he was hollering police brutality outside the theatre." My nose was bloody, my lips were cut and bleeding, and a four inch cut was on my left cheek trickling tiny drops of blood. My face was a puffy mess.

I collected my squad car from the alley behind the theatre where I had left it. En-route to City Hall, I went by Tenth and Patton where Tippit had been shot and killed. There, I saw his drying blood pooled in the street. The scene and the memory of J.D. made me very sad. Our Sergeant, Bud Owens, a twenty-five year man on the force was walking to his police car.

There were tears on his cheeks; he was crying silently, unashamed. I called to him, "I got him, Sarge!"

He continued walking with his head bowed, nodding wordlessly. This was too much; I was trying to hold back the tears as I drove to headquarters, but I was too sad and had that terrible, empty, remorseful feeling. I felt I knew what our whole country was experiencing at that very moment. Both our President and a fellow officer had been killed in cold blood.

12

THE LINK

AFTER REPORTING TO the crime lab and having my face photographed, I went to the homicide offices to get my handcuffs. The other officers had gone through the wallet of my prisoner and they had found identification of Alek James Hidell and Lee Harvey Oswald.

While I was asking about my handcuffs, Captain Will Fritz came out of his private office and told one of his detectives, "We need to get a warrant and go to Irving, and try to locate a missing employee of the Texas School Book Depository by the name of Lee Oswald."

"You don't have to do that. Lee Harvey Oswald is sitting right here!"

Suddenly, I realized not only had I apprehended the man responsible for the murder of Officer J.D. Tippit, but he may be a prime suspect in the assassination of President John F. Kennedy.

For the first time that day I felt elated. I had captured the assassin just ninety minutes after his dastardly deed. At approximately the same time that Vice President Lyndon B. Johnson was being sworn in as President of the United States of America, I was arresting the man accused of killing his predecessor. It was a great feeling of accomplishment and it was very difficult for me to comprehend the full significance of what I had done. Had it not been for J.D.'s chance confrontation with Oswald and Johnny Brewer's alertness to suspicious actions, this would not have been possible.

I also discovered that the handcuffs used on Oswald belong to Officer Ray Hawkins. I then checked my handcuff case and they had been there all along. I examined the pistol I had wrestled away from Oswald and it was fully loaded with six rounds of .38 caliber ammunition. Looking closely, the primer of one bullet was dented. My heart fell. I had felt the gun not fire in the theatre but now I was seeing it with my own eyes. Evidently, the web between my thumb and forefinger had retarded the firing pin on the hammer of his pistol so the primer on the shell did not receive the full striking force. Therefore, the bullet was not fired, which prevented me from getting shot.

Oswald's pistol was a Smith and Wesson .38 caliber revolver with a two-inch barrel, black finish, and wooden handles. For identification purposes when it would be introduced as evidence at Oswald's trial, I marked a small "mnm 11-22-63" on the butt of the pistol handle. I marked the same on each bullet that had been loaded in Oswald's revolver. A news photographer snapped a photo of me posing with Oswald's pistol.

I reported to Captain Westbrook's office to write the official report of my actions in arresting Oswald. When the reports were completed they were forwarded to Chief of Police Jesse E. Curry to be a part of the official records.

After completing the necessary report writing, I telephoned my wife, Sally, who was at work for an oil company. She answered crying, "The radio reported you had been shot and seriously wounded!"

I said, "No, I'm okay. I was not shot!" I tried to console and assure her, but she would not accept my words.

She said, "Let me speak to someone else!"

I handed the phone to Sergeant Hill and he told her, "Nick is safe and sound. He only has a few scrapes and scratches." She was unconvinced.

"I'm coming to headquarters to see for myself!" Sally replied.

When Sally arrived, I met her at the elevator and her tears were unrestrained and streaming down her cheeks. Wrapping my arms around her with a squeezing hug, I embraced her and held her close. Her tears of fear became happy tears when she realized I was still the same old cop. I could feel the cold dampness of her hand as she traced the cuts on my flushed face. As we were comforting each other I asked her to go home to be with our daughters. "Try to explain to them what happened and that I'm okay."

"You won't believe what has happened to me on this day!"

I said, "What happened?"

"Well, while we were all at the window watching the motorcade and the President someone went through my desk and stole my billfold. And, that's not all. On the way over here, I had a little accident."

"Are you okay?"

"Oh, it was just a fender bender and not that serious. The only trouble was my driver's license was in my billfold. But that's okay. I explained to the man what was happening, and who you were, and we exchanged names and phone numbers."

Captain Westbrook met me in the hallway just a few steps away from Captain Fritz's office and the interrogation room where they were questioning my prisoner. He said, "Your duties are finished for the day. You can go home now."

I returned to my squad car that I had left parked in the basement of City Hall. I drove back to the Oak Cliff Police Substation where I had began my day and tour of duty. I was met by my rookie partner patiently waiting for me. He refused to leave the station and go home until he was sure I was alright. He was a very loyal partner and I was prideful for his concern for my safety.

Alone and surrounded by solemnity in the now empty locker room, I changed to my street clothes. Hearing a slight noise, I turned and saw Officer J.L. Anglin and Allen Tippit, J.D.'s oldest son enter the locker room. They came to take J.D.'s personal car home to J.D.'s wife, Marie. I went up to Allen and gave him a gentle pat on his shoulder. I tried to hold back my tears and say something, but I was lost for words; none were needed—he understood.

Driving home I was disquieted, beginning to realize the full import of the tragedies which had taken place. When I arrived home it was 6:00 p.m. It had been a long day.

The night was even longer.

13

TWO CASES OF MURDER

THERE WAS AN atmosphere of sadness in the house. Sally and my daughters had what felt like a million questions about the day's events. I gathered them around me and tried to explain what had happened. But, how do you answer the most puzzling question: *why?*

A good neighbor had provided our dinner and brought it to us. They heard what had happened to me and wanted to show their kindness and gratitude for what I had done. Even though the food was delicious, we didn't have much of an appetite.

Doubt, suspicion, and curiosity kept us watching TV and listening to the radio, trying to keep abreast of the slightest developments from news flashes of the assassination. At 9:00 p.m. Sally and I went over to the Tippit's house to offer our condolences and sympathy to Marie and the children. They lived in the same neighborhood just down the street. Friends and other neighbors had gathered to help ease their loss, bringing food and comfort. The lights had been dimmed and the house was dark, casting shadows that surrounded us with a veil of grief.

This family had suffered the loss of a devoted husband and father; our department had lost a capable police officer. As we were leaving, Marie expressed her thanks to me for what I had done. Her voice was trembling as she tried to choke back the tears. I acknowledged her gratitude, nodding my head in sorrowful silence. I was experiencing firsthand what my family would have gone through had I not returned to them. I realized that Sally felt this even more; she saw Marie's devastation in her bereavement.

At home, our telephone rang constantly. Our friends were trying to find out how badly I had been hurt. They had heard the reports that I was wounded in the struggle and arrest of Oswald. My mother had been trying desperately to call from New England, but all the trunk lines to Dallas had been overwhelmed with calls from all over the world. Mother finally got through after telling the operator she was the mother of the police officer who had arrested the alleged assassin of President Kennedy. When we were connected, she acted like a mother by scolding me for placing myself in such a dangerous situation.

She said, "Are you alright? The news reported you had been shot and were wounded!"

Getting a word in, I said, "No, mother. I wasn't seriously injured. I'm fine and still okay." I told her not to worry. I don't know if I convinced her, but she did calm down when I tried to assure her I was safe and sound. "Remember, mom, I am a police officer and I do face danger once in a while, but I do try to use care," I explained.

We put the girls to bed. Our daughters were snug and safe breathing deeply in their peaceful sleep. At midnight, we turned off the TV and went to bed. Lying in our cozy bed, we listened to the radio for updated news bulletins. With each report of the mounting evidence against the suspected assassin, Lee Harvey Oswald, I was feeling more confident that he, and he alone, was responsible for the killings. When I heard that two cases of murder were filed on Oswald, I felt satisfied that I had captured the right man. I turned off my radio and went to sleep almost immediately.

14

ORDINARY COP

ALTHOUGH I FELL asleep almost immediately, I awoke suddenly. I felt I had slept the night away except it had only been about fifteen minutes. The events of the day had caught up with me, and my thoughts would not let me rest. After tossing and turning, morning finally came.

It was Saturday and the girls could sleep in. It was the day Sally devoted to housework and just another work day for me.

After Sally and I had our coffee, we said our *"see you laters."* I reported for duty as usual.

All the guys congratulated me on a job well done, but the noticeable absence of J.D. made the smiles much tougher to come by. His loss was felt all. At 10:00 a.m. my rookie partner, T.R. Gregory, and I received a radio call to a wrecking yard in west Dallas to investigate a couple of teenage boys who were attempting to sell a set of stolen hubcaps. The inside of the hubcaps were marked by the rightful owner and had been reported and identified as stolen. Our preliminary investigation revealed that the hubcaps were stolen earlier that morning. We confiscated the hubcaps, placed the boys under arrest, and transported them to the Juvenile Bureau for booking.

After we had completed the paperwork on the youths, I was confronted in the hall by a reporter. He requested an interview concerning the arrest of Oswald.

I began the interview by saying, "Yesterday I grabbed the guy they say shot the President and a police officer. Today, I arrested a couple of kids for stealing hubcaps. I guess that makes me just an ordinary cop." The life of an ordinary cop was doing the best job we could to preserve and protect. We start out each day with that in mind. No matter the job, we were expected to be our best. We had to make instant decisions that held up in the most exacting courts of law—even the highest court in the land.

Ordinary we may appear, but were anything but ordinary. We were called on daily to risk our lives for the protection of others. We did this without hesitating or thinking of our own safety first. When we left our homes, our loved ones feared we might never return. We just did it.

Each day before I left, I made it a point to kiss my wife and children. Their last words were always, "Be careful. We will see you later." *Never goodbye.* Their anxieties were my deep concern, and I always tried to be careful to make sure I returned safely.

15

OSWALD SHOT

THE NEXT DAY, November 24, was my regular day off. We decided the whole family should go to church that Sunday. I wanted to thank God, in His house, for protecting and guiding me throughout my chosen profession. After my near death experience, I knew that He was with me every step I had taken that day. He spared my life, and He was at my side during the desperate struggle with this man who had committed murder. God's will and the strength of my faith, contributed to my well being, as always.

As the minister was giving the benediction, a lay member came to his side and whispered. There was a hush throughout the congregation. Finally, the minister in a composed and sad voice announced, "Oswald has just been shot at City Hall." I was taken by surprise and bewildered.

I said out loud, "Oh, my God!" My first thought was that a policeman had shot him. Then I thought, all that I had tried to accomplish was now null and void.

I left the church in a daze, not really accepting it had actually happened. As we drove away the car radio was updating the shooting, reporting that Jack Ruby had fired the fatal shot. As Oswald was being transferred from the city jail to the county jail, Jack Ruby had stepped out of a crowd of reporters in the parking basement of the City Hall and shot Oswald. Thank God a policeman didn't shoot him. I thought to myself, *How did Jack Ruby get in the basement and how was he able to shoot Oswald?*

When we returned from church, I turned on the TV and saw the rerun of the murder that millions had witnessed as it happened. I couldn't believe it! A real live murder committed on national television. When it was announced that Oswald had expired at Parkland Hospital, I turned to Sally and said, "Well, Jack Ruby has just undone everything I tried to accomplish. If I had wanted him dead, I could have done that! There were too many unanswered questions for this to have happened."

Later I learned how Jack Ruby got in the basement and shot Oswald.

Saturday evening, sometime after 7:30 p.m., Chief Jesse E. Curry advised two reporters that if they returned to City Hall by 10:00 a.m. Sunday morning, they wouldn't miss the transfer of Oswald. At 10:20 a.m., Chief Curry told the press that Oswald would be moved in an armored truck but did not disclose the time or the route. The armored truck arrived at the Commerce Street exit of the basement at 11:07 a.m. Captain Fritz disagreed with Curry's plan and wanted to use an unmarked police car driven by a police officer. The armored truck was to be used as a decoy. The plan was for the armored truck to leave the ramp first, followed by a car which would contain only police officers. A police car bearing Oswald would then follow.[12]

Captain Fritz told Lieutenant Rio "Sam" Pierce to obtain another police car in the basement parking garage and take up the lead position on Commerce Street in front of the armored truck. Since the armored truck was blocking the Commerce Street ramp it would be necessary to drive out the wrong way on the Main Street entrance ramp. Lieutenant Pierce drove to the top of the Main Street ramp and slowed as Patrolman R.E. Vaughn left his position at the top of the ramp and went in the street to stop the traffic for Lieutenant Pierce's car.[13]

Jack Ruby lived in an apartment at 223 S. Ewing Street. On November 24th, he received a phone call at 10:19 a.m. from Karen Carlin, an entertainer, who was now in Fort Worth. She had worked for Ruby in his nightclub. She asked Ruby to send $25 to help her on the rent and buy groceries. Ruby told her he was going downtown and he would send the money by Western Union. After bathing and shaving, Ruby left his apartment a few minutes before 11:00 a.m. and took his dog and a portable radio with him.

Placing a revolver in his pocket, he drove downtown by a route that took him past Dealey Plaza and the county jail. He noticed a crowd had gathered outside the county jail and assumed that Oswald had already been transferred. When he passed the Main Street side of City Hall, which is in the same block as the Western Union office, he noticed a crowd had gathered outside City Hall.

Ruby parked his car in a parking lot directly across the street from Western Union. He placed his keys, along with his money bag and billfold in the trunk then locked the trunk and placed the trunk key in the glove compartment of the car. He arrived approximately fifteen minutes after leaving his apartment on Ewing Street.

With his revolver and more than $2,000 in cash, Ruby walked directly to the Western Union office. He filled out forms for sending $25 by telegraph to Karen Carlin. Ruby paid for the money order and kept his time-stamped receipt, which showed that the transaction was completed at 11:17 a.m.[14]

The Western Union clerk who accepted Ruby's order, saw that he promptly turned, walked out of the door on to Main

Street, and proceeded in the direction of the police department one block away.[15]

Jack Ruby got to the Main Street ramp just as Lieutenant Pierce was driving slowly out. Ruby, apparently unseen, turned in and walked down the ramp. When he got to the bottom, he edged into the crowd of reporters toward the front. Just as Ruby got there, the officers brought out Oswald. Ruby stepped out of the crowd and fired, shooting Oswald. The time was 11:21 a.m.

When Ruby saw Oswald, he took out his gun, pointed, and pulled the trigger. The police officers that had formed the security line wrestled Ruby to the floor and disarmed him. He cried out, "I am Jack Ruby. You all know me!" Later, Jack Ruby told a policeman the reason he shot Oswald was, "I was afraid that Mrs. Kennedy would be asked to return to Dallas for the trial! And, everyone will think of me as a hero for killing the man that killed the President!"[16]

16

JACK RUBY

I'VE KNOWN JACK Ruby over the years from reputation and personal contacts on different occasions. My first recollection was an encounter meeting about 3:00 a.m. in the morning in 1957. My partner and I were having breakfast at Lucas B&B Restaurant on Oak Lawn Avenue just a couple of doors from Jack Ruby's Vegas Club. We were in our police uniforms and Jack came over to our table and introduced himself. He was extraordinarily friendly and outgoing, inviting us to bring our wives or girlfriends to his club and said everything would be on him.

As we went to the cashier to pay, the cashier smiled and said, "Jack has already paid for your breakfast." I turned around to find Jack and give him the money for the check, but he had already left the restaurant.

One occasion, Sally and I had asked close friends to go out on the town. We took my childhood friend, Giles "Kitty" Katz, and his wife, Doris, out to dinner. After dinner, we went to the Vegas Club for dancing.

Jack Ruby came over to our table and introduced himself and speaking to me, said, "Aren't you a police officer that works Oak Cliff?"

"Yes."

Jack said, "I thought I recognized you from seeing you out in your patrol car in the neighborhood. Listen, everything is on the house. Have a good time! You guys don't get paid enough and I respect the work that you do."

I told him, "No, that's okay. We'll pay for our drinks. Thanks anyway."

The waitress refused our money, but we did leave a nice tip for her.

Several months later, my next encounter with Jack was a radio call to his apartment to report a theft at 3:00 a.m. Jack had allowed one of his acts at his club, a ventriloquist, to stay at his apartment while he was in town performing at his club. Someone had broken into the ventriloquist's car that had been parked in the apartment complex parking lot. Clothing and some the props used in his act had been taken. Jack was really upset because someone had the audacity to break in a car parked in his apartment parking lot.

The next time I saw Jack Ruby was in the summer of 1963. We were working late nights, 11:30 p.m. until 7:30 a.m. My partner and I had stopped at a coffee shop at 4:00 a.m. for breakfast and coffee. The door opened and Jack walked in.

Acknowledging each other, I said, "What are you doing out so late, or are you just getting up?"

He replied, "I was on my way home and stopped for a cup of coffee, I just closed up the Carrousel."

I had never been inside Jack's Carrousel Club because I never had an occasion to go. My police patrol was the West Oak Cliff area approximately ten miles away and I was never called for police business at his club. The club was in downtown Dallas and was there to attract tourist and others who were fascinated by strippers, which was the theme of the Carrousel.

The very next time I saw Jack Ruby was when he shot and killed Lee Harvey Oswald on national television. I didn't see Jack again until he was confined to the Dallas County Jail. I went up to see him for the sole purpose of asking him why he shot Oswald. I needed to know why Jack Ruby had killed Oswald. I wanted to see him face-to-face and hear for myself what he had to say. In December 1963, I went to the county jail to do just that.

The deputy sheriff jailer brought Ruby up to a holding room that was used by attorneys and investigating officers where I was waiting. It was a small, drab room with no other furniture except a table and a couple of chairs. The county jail itself was painted a battleship gray, chipped and scarred from the constant use by the prisoners and jailers. All jails looked and smelled the same way. The clanging of the shutting steel doors all had the same final echoing sound. Even visitors had temporary feelings of panic and urgency as the screws were turned.

The jailer unlocked and swung open the heavy steel door and Jack Ruby shuffled into the tiny room instead of with his usual confident walk. Even though he was without leg irons, his shuffling hinted he had been previously shackled.

The jailer said, "Just knock on the door when you are ready to leave!" and closed the door behind us.

Jack and I were left alone. No one else was in that small, confined, solitary space.

He wasn't wearing regular street shoes, instead he wore jail issue terrycloth slippers and white coveralls, the Dallas County Jail uniform for all prisoners. The collar of his coveralls was open and a small patch of black chest hairs peeked out. His total appearance seemed odd because I had never seen Jack in anything other than a dark business suit and tie. His dark hair was combed back, but when he turned to sit at the lone, bare table between the two of us, his hair was matted in the back as if he had been lying in his bunk and hadn't bothered to brush it.

Jack held out his hand to me in a friendly gesture. When I grasped his outstretched palm, it felt wet and cold to the touch. His handshake was limp and effeminate, just a slight touching of hands.

Greeting him, I said, "Hello, Jack. Do you remember me?"

"Yeah, you're Officer McDonald, aren't you? You're out of uniform and I didn't know you at first."

"Yes, Jack, that's right. How have they been treating you?"

Shifting his position slightly he managed a smile and replied, "Oh, I'm okay, I guess. The food isn't the best but that's good, I need to take off a little weight anyway."

Sitting and facing one another, Jack seemed to be friendly, but anxious and apprehensive in his demeanor and facial expression. I said, "Jack, the reason I came up to see you was to ask you why you shot and killed Oswald." Before he could answer me I added, "I could've killed him in the theater, but I didn't, even though for a moment I thought about it."

Without hesitating, Jack replied, "Well, the little son-of-a-bitch had a smirk on his face every time I saw him and I couldn't stand his arrogant attitude when he talked to the press! And, I really felt sorry for the Kennedy family and I didn't want Jackie Kennedy to come back to Dallas and go through the agony of the trial of that little pip-squeak!"

I said, "Jack, are you sure those were your only reasons?"

Nodding his head yes, I could see in his eyes that he was sorry for what he had done. His mood was forlorn and revealed an unspoken feeling of hopelessness, sadness, and seemed apologetic in a subdued tone. We both sat in silence for a moment and I didn't know what else to say to him.

Without another word from him, I got up from the table and said, "Thank you for seeing me. I'll see you later, Jack."

Just a figure of speech without any real meaning.

I walked to the jail door and lightly tapped to summon the jailer, leaving Jack alone at the table with his head in his hands. I was only with Jack for less than five minutes. That was the last time I saw or spoke to Jack Ruby. I wasn't really satisfied with his answers, but knowing Jack Ruby and of his aggressive attitude and past encounters with customers in his night clubs, I believed he must have thought the world would embrace him as a hero of the Kennedy assassination. And now the man who executed the assassin of the President faced the death penalty for his unlawful act.

Walking out of the county jail, I remembered that Jack Ruby had been at police headquarters where they brought Lee Harvey Oswald down to the line-up room. The press and television reporters swarmed in, shouting rapid fire questions at Oswald. Jack Ruby's photograph was taken among a group of reporters as he stood on a chair to get an unobstructed view of the circus-like atmosphere. He had the opportunity to observe and hear the spoken denials of Lee Harvey Oswald to a captivated television viewing audience.

Oswald had been paraded up and down the hallways and public elevators of police headquarters in full view of the general public and in front of reporters, photographers, and television cameras for the world to see. The idea of killing Oswald might have been born in Jack Ruby at that time. But, what he had done could not be undone. By taking the law in his own hands, Jack Ruby had been the sole judge and jury. Regardless of whom he was accused of killing, Oswald was entitled to a fair trial in a court of law.

Ruby had denied him that right and privilege.

Jack Ruby hired two local attorneys to represent him, Chief Defense Counsel Clayton Fowler and Defense Counsel Joe H. Tonahill. Before his trial, Ruby hired Melvin Belli.

Jack Ruby's Previous Law Violations and Arrest Records:

Between 1949 and November 24, 1963, Ruby was arrested eight times by the Dallas Police Department. The dates, charges, and dispositions of these arrests are as follows:

February 4, 1949: Ruby paid a $10 fine for disturbing the peace.

July 26, 1953: Ruby was suspected of carrying a concealed weapon; however, no charges were filed and Ruby was released on the same day.

May 1, 1954: Ruby was arrested for allegedly carrying a concealed weapon and violating a peace bond; again no charges were filed and Ruby was released on the same day.

December 5, 1954: Ruby was arrested for allegedly violating state liquor laws by selling liquor after hours; the complaint was dismissed on February 8, 1955.

June 21, 1959: Ruby was arrested for allegedly permitting dancing after hours; the complaint was dismissed on July 8, 1959.

August 21, 1960: Ruby was again arrested for allegedly permitting dancing after hours; Ruby posted $25 bond and was released on that date.

February 12, 1963: Ruby was arrested on a charge of simple assault; he was found not guilty on February 27, 1963.

March 14, 1963: Ruby was arrested for allegedly ignoring traffic summonses; a $35 bond was posted.

Between 1950 and 1963, Ruby received twenty traffic tickets for motor vehicle violations. In 1956 and again in 1959, he was placed on six months' probation as a traffic violator.

Jack Ruby was also frequently suspended by the Texas Liquor Control Board. In August 1949, when he was operating the Silver Spur, he was suspended for five days on a charge of "Agents—Moral Turpitude." In 1953, Ruby received a five-day suspension because of an obscene show and in 1954, a ten-day suspension for allowing a drunkard on his premises. On February 10, 1954, he was suspended for five days because of an obscene striptease act at the Silver Spur and for the consumption of alcoholic beverages during prohibited hours.

On March 26, 1956, Ruby was suspended by the liquor board for three days because several of his checks were dishonored. On October 23, 1961, Ruby received a three-day suspension because an agent solicited the sale of alcoholic beverages for consumption on licensed premises.[17]

By Ruby's previous arrest records and law violations, no favoritism or special consideration was given to Jack by any law enforcement agencies. There was not a suggestion of double standards being a practice in Jack Ruby's records. He was fined and convicted in the majority of the charges filed against him. He never asked for special treatment or privileges. He always made it a point to be on good terms with law enforcement officials, hoping they would give him the benefit of the doubt if a questionable situation should arise.

Ruby always tried to keep in excellent physical condition. He frequently exercised at the YMCA, the Carousel, and his apartment where he kept a set of weights. He was extremely concerned about his weight and health including his receding hair line and his appearance in general. Ruby's concern for his physical well-being was partially motivated by practical considerations. He was his own club bouncer. On about fifteen occasions since 1950, he beat with his fist, pistol whipped, or blackjacked patrons who became unruly. Many people thought that he employed more force than necessary as he often ended a fracas by throwing his victims down the stairs of his Carousel Club.[18]

Besides acting as a bouncer, Ruby on numerous occasions severely beat people usually employing only his fists. In 1951, he attacked a man who had called him a "kike Jew" and knocked out the man's tooth. At about that time, Ruby was reported to have knocked a man down from behind and then kicked him in the face. In 1958, Ruby reportedly knocked down a man at the Vegas Club who was six foot three and two hundred thirty pounds. Ruby was approximately five foot nine and one hundred seventy-five pounds. Ruby then made the man, who had slapped his date, crawl out of the club on his hands and knees. In a fight at the Vegas Club, he severely beat a heavyweight boxer who had threatened him.[19]

During 1962, several other violent episodes occurred. Ruby beat a man who refused to pay admission or leave and then shoved him down the stairs. He "jostled" a woman down the stairs of the Carousel Club and struck her escort, who was "much smaller" than him. On another occasion, Ruby picked up a man who was arguing with his date, knocked him to the floor, cursed him, and then removed him from the Vegas Club. When a cabdriver entered the Carousel and inquired about a patron who had failed to pay his fare, Ruby struck the cabdriver.[20]

In February, 1963, Ruby badly beat Don Tabon who had made some remarks about Ruby's lady companion, and injured Tabon's eye. Ruby was acquitted of assault and Tabon sought no monetary relief because he believed Ruby was financially incapable of satisfying any resulting judgment.[21]

Buddy Turman, a professional prizefighter and Ruby's friend and bouncer at the Vegas Club, stated that Jack "picked his shots." Ruby's victims were either drunk, female, or otherwise incapable of successfully resisting Ruby's attack. While Ruby often flared up and acted aggressively, he calmed down or forgot his anger quickly, and there was evidence that he was generous to his friends. He loaned them money and apparently cared little whether the loans would be repaid. He was quick to offer employment to persons desperately in need of a job. When friends or acquaintances had no roof over their heads, Ruby's apartment was frequently theirs to share.[22]

Ruby's unusual generosity may be explained in part by his extremely emotional reaction to persons in distress, which may have resulted from his firsthand familiarity with poverty, and by his unusual craving to be recognized and relied upon. Many of his acquaintances described him as a publicity hound, glad hander, and name dropper; one always seeking to be the center of attention. Apparently, the egocentrism of his youth never left him. Yet, he sought reassurance from persons he admired.[23]

As I said before, my personal contacts and knowledge of Jack Ruby were more from a professional point of view. With my first professional contact with Jack, I could understand his willingness to be friendly; the simple fact that his business success depended on good, cooperative relationships with law enforcement in general. In Texas, it was a known fact for anyone to keep and maintain a liquor license, it was essential to have the enforcement officials on your side. In most cases, the attitude of any person to a police officer was the primary factor of any action he may or may not take.

THE WARREN COMMISSION'S INVESTIGATIONS RELATING TO JACK RUBY CONCLUDED THESE FACTS:

POLICE ASSOCIATIONS[24]

Although the precise nature of his relationships to members of the Dallas Police Department is not susceptible of conclusive evaluation, the evidence indicates that Ruby was keenly interested in policemen and their work. Jesse Curry, Chief of the Dallas Police Department, testified that no more than twenty-five to fifty of Dallas' almost 1,200 policemen were acquainted with Ruby. However, the reports of present and past members of the Dallas Police Department as well as Ruby's employees and acquaintances indicate that Ruby's police friendships were far more widespread than those of the average citizen.

There is no credible evidence that Ruby sought special favors from police officers or attempted to bribe them. Although there is considerable evidence that Ruby gave policemen reduced rates, declined to exact any cover charge from them, and gave them free coffee and soft drinks, his hospitality was not unusual for a Dallas nightclub operator. Ruby's personal attachment to police officers is demonstrated by reports that he attended the funeral of at least one policeman killed in action and staged a benefit performance for the widow of another. Ruby regarded several officers as personal friends, and others had worked for him. Finally, at least one policeman regularly dated, and eventually married, one of the Carousel's strippers.

Possible Assistance to Jack Ruby in Entering The Basement

The killing of Lee Harvey Oswald in the basement of police headquarters in the midst of more than seventy police officers gave rise to immediate speculation that one or more members of the police department provided Jack Ruby assistance which enabled him to enter the basement and approach within a few feet of the accused Presidential assassin.

In Chapter VI, the Commission considered whether there was any evidence linking Jack Ruby with a conspiracy to kill the President. At this point, however, it is appropriate to consider whether there is evidence that Jack Ruby received assistance from Dallas policemen or others in gaining access to the basement on the morning of November 24. An affirmative answer would require that the evidence be evaluated for possible connection with the assassination itself. While the Commission found no evidence that Ruby received assistance from any person in entering the basement, his means of entry is significant in evaluating the adequacy of the precautions taken to protect Oswald.

Although more than a hundred policemen and newsmen were present in the basement of police headquarters during the ten minutes before the shooting of Oswald, none has been found who definitely observed Jack Ruby's entry into the basement. After considering all the evidence, the Commission concluded that Ruby entered the basement unaided, probably via Main Street ramp, and no more than three minutes before the shooting of Oswald.

Ruby's account of how he entered the basement by the Main Street ramp merits consideration in determining his means of entry. Three Dallas policemen testified that approximately thirty minutes after his arrest, Ruby told them that he had walked to the top of the Main Street ramp from the nearby Western Union office and that he walked down the ramp at the time the police car driven by Lieutenant Pierce emerged into Main Street. This information did not come to light immediately because the policemen did not report it to their superiors until some days later. Ruby refused to discuss his means of entry in interrogations with other investigators later on the day of his arrest. Thereafter, in a lengthy interview on December 21 and in a sworn deposition taken after his trial, Ruby gave the same explanation he had given to the three policemen.

The Commission has been able to establish with precision the time of certain events leading up to the shooting. Minutes before Oswald appeared in the basement, Ruby was in the Western Union office located on the same block of Main Street, some three hundred and fifty feet from the top of the Main Street ramp. The time stamp on a money order established that the order was accepted for transmission at almost exactly 11:17 a.m. Ruby was then observed departing the office and walking without interruption in the direction of the police building. One hundred forty-three video tapes taken without interruption before the shooting establish that Lieutenant Pierce's car cleared the crowd at the foot of the ramp fifty-five seconds before the shooting. They also show Ruby standing at the foot of the ramp on the Main Street side before the shooting. The shooting occurred very close to 11:21 a.m. This time has been established by observing the time on a clock appearing in motion pictures of Oswald in the basement jail office, and by records giving the time of Oswald's departure from the city jail and the time at which an ambulance was summoned for Oswald.

The Main Street ramp provided the most direct route to the basement from the Western Union office. At normal stride, it requires approximately one minute to walk from that office to the top of Main Street ramp and about twenty to twenty-five seconds to descend the ramp. It is certain, therefore, that Ruby entered the basement no more than two to three minutes before the shooting. This timetable indicates that a little more than two of the four minutes between Ruby's departure from the Western Union office and the time in loitering along the way, at the top of the ramp, or inside the basement. However, if Ruby is correct that he passed Pierce's car at the top of the ramp, he could have been in the basement no more than thirty seconds before the shooting.

The testimony of two witnesses partially corroborates Ruby's claim that he entered by the Main Street ramp.

James Turner, an employee of WBAP-TV Fort Worth, testified that while he was standing near the railing on the east side of Main Street ramp, perhaps thirty seconds before the shooting, he observed a man he is confident was Jack Ruby moving slowly down the Main Street ramp about ten feet from the bottom. Two other witnesses testified that they thought they had seen Ruby on the Main Street side of the ramp before the shooting.

17

MARINA IN LATER YEARS

I HAD NOT heard about Marina for several years until my daughter, Michelle, called me and said she had met Marina who was working at a 7-11 store in north Dallas. Michelle had been working near Spring Valley and Coit Road and at lunch time she went to 7-11 to get a Coke. Low and behold, working behind the counter was none other than Marina Oswald. Her telephone call had really surprised me.

Michelle related how she went to the counter to pay for her Coke and how the lady looked just like Marina Oswald from the television and newspaper stories. Michelle asked if she was her and she said she had remarried and her name was now Marina Porter.

Michelle explained I was her father and asked if she remembered me. Marina said, "Oh, yes. He was a very kind man. Tell him, I said hello. He was very kind to me and my daughters."

I could not believe Marina Oswald had come to this, a clerk in a 7-11 store after all that happened! I said, "It's really too bad that she had to take a job like that after receiving all that money from the American people."

Another experience relating to Marina was a complete surprise to me. It was unexpected and I was taken aback. On Easter Sunday after attending church services, a group of fellow church members suggested going out to eat at a local restaurant for an Easter brunch. A visiting couple was invited to come along. Mr. and Mrs. David Lundberg of Dallas were in Hot Springs preparing to retire. I went to their table and introduced myself and welcomed them to our community. After they had settled in their new home on beautiful Lake Catherine, they joined the church and we became close friends because of the common bond we shared being from Dallas. We became good friends to David and Katherine. David and I were both golf hackers, playing many rounds at a local country club.

Katherine said out of the blue that someone told her I was a retired Dallas police officer, and had arrested the accused assassin, Lee Harvey Oswald. She then related how she had known Marina Oswald Porter, and had been good friends. These are Katherine Lundberg's words as she remembered:

"I met Marina Oswald Porter the summer of 1974 at a 7-11 store which was managed by my then boyfriend, Bruce Freeman. He had a store a block from Marina's apartment; I also had a 7-11 in the opposite direction. She was one of his clerks and he asked me to take her into my store because he was finding it difficult to communicate with her—no language difficulty, just a personality conflict. Bruce told me what he knew of her history, including the fact that she lived with her two daughters and that she had no car. She was divorced from Kenneth Porter and their son was living with him.

"When I met Marina, I liked her immediately. She was courteous, cheerful, petite and cute, and agreed to come and work for me. Marina worked the midnight shift in my store, arriving for work around 10:30 p.m. and leaving to get her girls ready for school at 7:00 a.m. Marina loved to visit with the workers from Texas Instruments that came in the store for break to play pinball machines and eat snacks. She was a wonderful hostess to the guests, but didn't do much of the back up work, mopping, stocking shelves, or price changes during her shift. After getting her girls off to school, Marina walked back to the store and spent another two or three hours doing those chores off the clock, and then walked back to her apartment. She asked for my permission to follow that schedule, saying she didn't like to be back in the rear of the store at night, and she enjoyed being with customers.

"I never asked Marina any questions about her former marriages or life, though she eventually began telling me parts of her past history. I'd take her home when the weather was bad and she'd invite me in. Sometimes, we'd just talk; sometimes, she'd show me photos. As we grew closer, she told me several things about her stormy marriage to Lee, including that he beat and kicked her when she was pregnant trying to make her lose her babies. It seems she told me she had one miscarriage, but I'm not sure about that. Lee didn't allow her to learn to speak English, or leave the house without him or his mother. She told me that after the assassination there was a fund set up for her and the girls and she was very grateful for all the contributions from the citizens of the U.S. At one point, however, she felt that the public, because they had donated to the "poor little Russian Widow" owned her and that she was supposed to "check in" and give regular reports. She began to resent that, as well as the newspaper articles that told of her smoking "menthol cigarettes" (Kools) and laughing like she should be ashamed to do something so normal and carefree.

"At the end of October 1974, Bruce Freeman and I were married. Bruce did not want anyone at our marriage, but as we had grown close (Marina was my only friend in Dallas), he allowed me to invite Marina. She stood up with me as my matron of honor. My mother-in-law (another 7-11 store manager) gave us a small luncheon after the marriage ceremony and the three of us went. Marina told us that she loved Kenneth Porter and regretted leaving him. Bruce's mother, Marina, and I went out one evening for a drive, and Marina spoke of her domestic situation and Mrs. Freeman, basing her advice on her own regrets about a failed marriage, counseled her to go back to Mr. Porter if he still loved her. After listening, Marina said that the advice was what she needed and that she would return; she gave notice and left the employ of Southland Corporation shortly thereafter. I only spoke to Marina once or twice later. I found out that she worked at a mall dress store. I called her there and told her that I had had a baby. I never tried to contact her again, mostly to give her the privacy she sought so much. I didn't realize that our friendship might have been a blessing to her as well as to me—I just thought that she'd think I was calling because she had begun to be in the news again and I didn't want to bother her."

IN JANUARY 1998, I received a phone call from Marina Oswald Porter. Earlier, I had written her a letter asking if we could get together and talk about old times. I had planned to be in the Dallas area next week. Instead of answering my letter, she decided to telephone me. I was totally unprepared and surprised to hear from her. My plans were to have a photograph taken of us together. But, she told me we would only argue and did not want to see me at her job. She was working at an army-navy store in Dallas at that time.

Our conversation was mostly one-sided. She wanted to berate me for calling Lee a communist and an assassin, that I was wrong to say Lee was guilty of assassinating President Kennedy. She also disagreed about everything I said on the television program "Top Cops." She rambled endlessly about how Lee was just a "patsy" involved in a cover-up by the Warren Commission and a conspiracy with unknown persons. Others were involved and Lee was just doing as he was told by others, not named.

When I questioned her about Lee's attempt on General Walker's life and the note Lee had left behind giving her instructions on what to do if he was arrested, she replied, "Others were involved and I was just a young, innocent twenty-two year old Russian girl and I didn't realize what was going on around me!"

"Why did Lee try to kill me when I arrested him?"

"Lee was just running scared and was protecting himself." She even denied that Lee killed J.D. Tippit, saying, "It was never proven." I tried to tell her of the evidence proving Lee had shot Tippit, but she discredited everything I said as I tried to explain the proven facts to her. I let her ramble on and on. I even went as far to tell her that I did not connect the killing of Officer Tippit and the assassination of President Kennedy until later, when it was discovered Lee was the missing employee of the Texas School Book Depository soon after the assassination. Marina just ignored everything I said. Personally, I believe she has been brainwashed with conspiracy theories.

She asked if Jim Martin's residence was a safe house. I explained it was a safe house for her and her daughters, and we were there to keep her safe so she would be able to testify before the Warren Commission. She was also curious about Jim Martin and where he might be today. She thought he was a "plant" by the Secret Service or the FBI. Marina kept telling me that she wished Lee had been guilty so she could put away all doubts. I kept telling her there was physical evidence, and people at a bus stop at Tenth and Patton identified her husband from a police lineup as the man that had gunned down J.D. Tippit.

She wanted to know if I had read all twenty-six volumes of the Warren Report. I told her no, but what I knew was from my personal experience and the unchallenged facts of the discovered evidence of the guns used in the crimes leading directly to Lee. She again answered, "Lee was just scared!" Marina said, "She thought I was just doing my job in arresting Lee and she did not think badly of me or for what I had done in arresting Lee." Adding, "Lee did not resist arrest!"

Then I asked Marina, "Where did I get a bloody face and a scar that still remains on my face to this day, if he did not resist?"

She replied, "He was just protecting himself from police brutality." Most of the things she was telling me was repetitious and rambling about how Lee was just a 'patsy' and was innocent. Marina said, "I'm 57 years old now and was getting too old to worry about it anymore and all that had happened was a long, long time ago."

I could not convince her that Oswald had committed these crimes. But she still maintains that there were persons unknown behind the conspiracy and Lee was just a 'patsy' and doing as he was told to do.

Ending the conversation, Marina told me she had remembered my daughter, Michelle, when she came in the 7-11 where she was working a long time ago. In an interview with Jack Anderson of *Ladies Home Journal,* Marina said she was used by the Warren Commission. "I was young, immature and naive. At the time I was asked questions that suit the theory of a single assassin. Now I believe there was a conspiracy, that more than one person was involved. I do not necessarily believe that the bullet that came from the depository shot President Kennedy. I don't know if Lee shot him. I'm not saying Lee is innocent, that he didn't know about the conspiracy or was not a part of it, but I am saying that he's not necessarily guilty of murder...I think he was caught between two powers—the government and organized crime. Someone may have wanted Kennedy killed, but who was supposed to do what, I don't know."

This telephone call was in 1988. Even today, she still believes that Lee Harvey Oswald was a "patsy."

18

WARREN COMMISSION

WHEN I RECEIVED notice to appear before the Warren Commission, I sat down with my wife, Sally, and our two children, and read the subpoena to them. My oldest daughter, Vicki, said, "Daddy, be sure and tell them how that bad old man tried to kill you in the picture show!" I told her I would.

On the commercial plane to Washington, D.C., there were four police officers summoned to appear before the Warren Commission to hear our testimonies. Two Dallas County Deputy Sheriffs, Luke Mooney and Eugene Boone, and two Dallas Police Officers, Marrion L. Baker and me, M.N. "Nick" McDonald. The two deputies sat in the seats directly behind Baker and me.

Deputy Eugene Boone testified where he had found the rifle used by Oswald on the sixth floor of the Texas School Book Depository. Deputy Luke Mooney was to testify that he discovered the southeast corner firing site and had joined Deputy Boone shortly after Boone and Deputy Constable Seymour Weitzman found the Mannlicher-Carcano rifle hidden among the cardboard boxes on the sixth floor.

Of course, I testified to the arrest and capture of Lee Harvey Oswald. On the other hand, Marrion Baker's testimony, as he told me, was more detailed in his actions that day.

Marrion L. Baker loved to hunt and he was very familiar with the sounds of rifle fire. He was riding his motorcycle in front of Chief of Police Jesse Curry's lead car. He was making his turn on to Elm Street from Houston Street and was about halfway to the intersection when he heard three loud exploding rifle shots. He jerked his motorcycle to the curb and jumped off, running toward the Elm and Houston intersection where he believed the shots had originated. Looking up, he saw pigeons scattering from the roof of the Texas School Book Depository building. The shots produced echoes probably caused by other tall buildings. Baker reached the front of the Texas School Book Depository and pushed his way through the crowd of frightened, confused people gathered at the entrance. As Baker walked inside he called out, "Who's in charge here?"

"I'm Roy Truly, building manager," he told Baker.

"Come with me. I want to look on the roof. That's where I think the shots came from."

Baker turned to the other people at the door. "Don't let anyone out of the building. More officers will be here in a minute to help."

Baker followed Truly through a hallway that led to the rear of the building where Truly pressed his hands against the closed elevator doors. "I guess both elevators are upstairs. Come on, it will be quicker if we walk."

They dashed up the wooden stairs. At the second floor landing Baker stopped to catch his breath and through the glass window of the door leading to the second floor lunchroom, he spotted a man walking toward the other end of the room. Baker opened the door and drew his pistol. "Come here," he ordered, and the man turned and approached him. He was thin, young and empty-handed.

"Do you know him?" Baker shouted to Truly.

"Yeah. He's one of my men. Name's Oswald. He's an order filler."

Baker put his gun back in his holster and with Truly started up another flight of stairs. Roy Truly's quick response to Baker's question caused Baker to dismiss any suspicion or other inquiry and questions he might have asked during this face-to-face chance meeting of Oswald.

A special car picked us up at Dulles Airport and took us to the Willard Hotel. Baker and I shared a room. The next morning the car picked us up again and took us to the Supreme Court Building where the Warren Commission was having the hearings. We were on the second floor waiting to be called. We were dressed in civilian suits and I was armed with my pistol, holstered onto my belt. I checked with the officer sitting at a desk next to the door of the Hearing Room. I wanted him to be aware I was armed, and wanted to know if I should check it with him before I went inside the Hearing Room.

He shook his head, indicating no and said, "It's okay. You are a police officer aren't you?" With that, I returned to my seat and continued to wait to be called.

While waiting, Chief Justice Earl Warren came up to me and introduced himself and said, "Officer McDonald, I want to congratulate you on a fine job you did down in Dallas. We are all very proud of you!"

I got to my feet and grasped his extended hand and I shook it as firm as I dared to squeeze. "Thank you Mr. Chief Justice, I appreciate it very much."

He explained, "I must leave on important business and I will not hear your testimony, but I did want to meet you." I was in awe of meeting such a great and powerful man. Soon afterward, I was called into the Hearing Room. I entered the room and the first thing I noticed was a long conference table. Attorneys and members of the Commission were seated on both sides and at one end. At the end of the room, the Attorney General of Texas, Waggoner Carr, was seated at a large desk, taking notes. At the other side of the room, the official historian was also busy taking notes.

Taking a look around the table, those in attendance were Senators Richard B. Russell, John Sherman Cooper, Representative Gerald R. Ford, Attorneys Joseph A. Ball, David W. Belin, and other staff members.

An attorney said, "Officer McDonald, be seated, please."

There were two chairs which were unoccupied; a huge padded leather chair at the side and a simple office chair placed at the end of the conference table. Being a bit nervous, tense and apprehensive, I sat down in the large leather chair. Everybody was smiling, and the attorney said, "Not there, that's Chief Justice Warren's chair. Sit in the other one, please." Embarrassed, I smiled and gave a quick apology.

Sitting down in the proper chair, I tried to compose myself for the inquisition.

It was the most thorough questioning I had ever known. They went step-by-step from the time I responded to the call at the Texas Theatre, until Oswald was handcuffed and taken out of the theatre.

Mr. Ball, began his questioning:

Q. What did you do?

A. Well, when I got to the front of the theater there was several police cars already at the scene, and I surmised that officers were already inside the theater. So I decided to go to the rear... There were three other officers at the rear door. I joined them. We walked into the rear exit door over the alley.

Q. What were their names?

A. Officer Hawkins, T.A. Hudson, and C.T. Walker. And as we got inside the door, we were met by a man that was in civilian clothes, a suit, and he told us that the man that acted suspiciously as he ran into the theatre was sitting downstairs in the orchestra seats. He was sitting at the rear of the theatre alone. Officer Walker and I went to the exit curtains that is to the left of the movie screen. I looked into the audience; I saw a person that the shoe store salesman had pointed out to us.

Q. Were the lights on or off?

A. The lights were up, and the movie was playing at this time.

Q. And you could see to the rear of the theatre?

A. Yes, sir. As I got to the row where the suspect was sitting, I stopped abruptly, and turned in and told him to get on his feet. He rose immediately, bringing up both hands.

He got his hand about shoulder high, and he got his right hand about breast high. He said, "Well it's all over now." As he said this, I put my left hand on his waist and then his right hand went to his waist. And this hand struck me between the eyes on the bridge of the nose.

Q. Did he cock his fist?

A. Yes, sir; knocking my cap off.

Q. Which fist did he hit you with?

A. His left fist.

Q. What happened then?

A. Well, whenever he knocked my hat off, any normal reaction was for me to go at him with this hand.

Q. Right hand?

A. Yes, I struck him with this hand, and I believe I struck him in the face, but I don't know where. And with my hand, that was on his hand over the pistol.

Q. Did you feel the pistol?

A. Yes, sir.

Q. Was his right hand or his left hand on the pistol?

A. His right hand was on the pistol.

Q. And which of your hands?

A. My left hand, at this point.

Q. And had he withdrawn the pistol?

A. He was drawing it as I put my hand...

Q. From his waist?

A. Yes, sir.

Q. What happened then?

A. Well, whenever I hit him, we both fell into the seats. While we were struggling around there, with his hand on the gun—

Q. Your left hand?

A. Yes, sir. Somehow I managed to get this hand in the action also.

Q. Your right hand?

A. Yes, sir. Now, as we fell into the seats, I called out, "I've got him," and Officer T.A. Hudson, he came to the row behind us and grabbed Oswald around the neck. And then Officer C.T. Walker came into the row that we were in and grabbed his left arm. And Officer Ray Hawkins came to the row in front of us and grabbed him from the front. By the time all three of these officers had got there, I had gotten my right hand on the butt of the pistol and jerked it free.

Q. Had you felt any movement of the hammer?

A. Yes, sir. When this hand—we went down into the seats.

Q. When your left hand went into the seats, what happened?

A. It felt like something had grazed across my hand. I felt movement there. And that was the only movement I felt. And I heard a snap, I didn't know what it was at the time.

Q. Was the pistol out of his waist at that time?

A. Yes, sir.

Q. Did you know any way it was pointed?

A. Well, I believe the muzzle was toward me, because the sensation came across this way. To make movement like that, it would have to be the cylinder or the hammer.

Q. Across your left palm?

A. Yes, sir. And my hand was directly over the pistol in this manner. More or less the butt. But not on the butt.

Q. What happened when you jerked the pistol free?

A. When I jerked it free, I was down in the seats with him, with my head, some reason or other, I don't know why, and when I brought the pistol out, it grazed me across the cheek here, and I put it all the way out to the aisle, holding it by the butt. I gave the pistol to Detective Bob Carroll at that point.

Q. Grazed your left cheek?

A. Yes, sir.

Q. Scratched—noticeable scratch?

A. Yes, sir; about a four-inch scratch just above the eye to just above the lip.

Q. Then what happened after that?

A. Well, the officers that had come to my aid started handcuffing him and taking him out of the theatre.

Q. What did he say—anything?

A. Well, he was cursing a little bit and hollering police brutality, for one thing.

Q. What words did he use?

A. I couldn't recall the exact words. It was just mixed up words, people hollering and screaming when they get arrested.

Q. What did he say about police brutality?

A. One thing, "Don't hit me anymore." I remember that.

Q. Did somebody hit him?

A. Yes, sir, I guess they did.

Q. Who hit him, do you know?

A. No, sir; I don't other than myself.

Q. You know you hit him?

A. Yes, sir.[25]

The Warren Commission Conclusion Concerning Oswald's Arrest

The Texas Theatre is on the north side of Jefferson Boulevard, approximately eight blocks from the scene of the Tippit shooting and six blocks from where several witnesses last saw Oswald running west on Jefferson Boulevard. Shortly after the Tippit murder, police sirens sounded along Jefferson Boulevard. One of the persons who heard the sirens was Johnny Calvin Brewer, manager of Hardy's shoe store, a few doors east of the Texas Theatre. Brewer knew from radio broadcasts that the President had been shot and that a patrolman had also been shot in Oak Cliff. When he heard police sirens, he "looked up and saw a man enter the lobby," a recessed area extending about fifteen feet from between the sidewalk and the front door of his store.

A police car made a U-turn, and as the sirens grew fainter, the man in the lobby "looked over his shoulder and walked up West Jefferson Boulevard toward the theatre." The man wore a T-shirt beneath his outer shirt and had no jacket. Brewer said, "He just looked funny to me. His hair was sort of messed up and looked like he had been running, and he looked scared, and he looked funny."

Mrs. Julia Postal, selling tickets at the box office of the Texas Theatre, heard police sirens and then saw a man as he "ducked into" the outer lobby space of the theatre near the ticket office. Attracted by the sound of the sirens, Mrs. Postal stepped out of the box office and walked to the curb. Shortly thereafter, Johnny Brewer, who had come from the nearby shoe store, asked Mrs. Postal whether the fellow that had ducked in bought a ticket. She said, "No; by golly, he didn't," and turned around, but the man was nowhere in sight.

Brewer told Mrs. Postal that he had seen the man ducking into his place of business and that he had followed him to the theatre. She sent Brewer into the theatre to find the man and check the exits, told him about the assassination, and said, "I don't know if this is the man they want, but he is running from them for some reason." Mrs. Postal then called the police.

At 1:45 p.m., the police radio stated, "Have information a suspect just went into the Texas Theatre on West Jefferson."

Patrol cars bearing at least fifteen officers converged on the Texas Theatre. Patrolman M.N. McDonald, with Patrolman R. Hawkins, T.A. Hutson, and C.T. Walker, entered the theatre from the rear. Other policemen entered the front door and searched the balcony. Detective Paul Bentley rushed the balcony and told the projectionist to turn up the house lights. Brewer met McDonald and the other policemen at the alley exit door, stepped out onto the stage with them, and pointed out the man who had come into the theatre without paying.

The man was Oswald. He was sitting alone in the rear of the main floor of the theatre near the right center aisle. About six or seven people were seated on the theatre's main floor and an equal number in the balcony.

McDonald first searched two men in the center of the main floor, about ten rows from the front. He walked out of the row up to the right center aisle. When he reached the row where the suspect was sitting, McDonald stopped abruptly and told the man to get on his feet. Oswald rose from his seat, bringing up both hands. As McDonald started to search Oswald's waist, he heard him say, "Well, it's all over now." Oswald then struck McDonald between the eyes with his left fist; with his right hand he drew a gun from his waist. McDonald struck back with his right hand and grabbed the gun with his left hand. They both fell into the seats. Three other officers, moving toward the scuffle, grabbed Oswald from the front, rear and side. As McDonald fell into the seats with his left hand on the gun, he felt something graze across his hand and heard what sounded like the snap of the hammer. McDonald felt the pistol scratch his cheek as he wrenched it away from Oswald. Detective Bob Carroll, who was standing beside McDonald, seized the gun from him.[26]

AFTER THE QUESTIONING was over and I was excused, I was honored when Senator John Sherman Cooper of Kentucky asked if he could have his photograph taken with me by a *Washington Post* newspaper photographer.

Senator Cooper said, "Congratulations on a job well done." Then he handed me ten newly minted Kennedy half-dollars. I was thrilled because that very day was March 25, 1964, the same day I testified before the Warren Commission.

All four of us testified that day. Dallas Police Motorcycle Officer Marrion L. Baker was one of the motorcycle escorts in the presidential motorcade. Officer Baker was with Mr. Roy S. Truly, superintendent of the Texas School Book Depository, when he first confronted Oswald at the Coke machine located on the second floor of the building, but was advised by Mr. Truly that Oswald was an employee. At the time, Officer Baker did not consider Oswald suspect because Mr. Truly vouched for his employee.

The third officer was Deputy Sheriff of Dallas County Luke Mooney. Deputy Mooney discovered three empty cartridge cases on the floor near the opened window on the sixth floor.

Deputy Sheriff of Dallas County Eugene Boone was the fourth officer. He found the rifle with the mounted scope, partially hidden between two rows of boxes in the northwest corner near the staircase on the sixth floor.

After my testimony, lasting approximately two hours, and the other officers had completed, we all went out to dinner—on the government I might add—at one of Washington's finest restaurants. Bright and early the next morning, we were again chauffeured to the airport. We returned to Dallas and I to my family, and my duties as an ordinary cop. The difference was I was in plainclothes but still just an ordinary cop.

When the Warren Commission Report was completed and published for the general public, there was criticism and controversy. Almost everyone had questions and did not fully support the findings as a factual report or completely believe a lone assassin was responsible.

I had direct orders and instructions from my superiors to maintain a low profile and I was not to discuss any aspects of the Warren Commission Report and their findings.

19

THE INFAMOUS ZAPRUDER FILM

THE TWENTY-SIX SECONDS of an 8mm color film taken by Abraham Zapruder was one of the most important aids in the investigation of President Kennedy's assassination. Of all the films taken and analyzed, the one by Abraham Zapruder contained the most precise detail of determination than any other film capturing this moment in history.

According to the Warren Commission Report, based on Zapruder's film, the speed of the President's limousine was computed at an average speed of 11.2 miles per hour and maintained this average speed over a distance of approximately 136 feet. Over this distance, the Zapruder camera ran 152 frames and it was calculated the limousine required 8.3 seconds to cover the 136 feet. This represented a speed of 11.2 miles per hour of the President's automobile. The frames of the film correlate the shots fired with the movements in the President's car.

Without the film of the assassination, the investigation would have depended on eyewitness accounts and testimonies, which in my opinion would be faulty in many instances. No two witnesses have ever agreed on what they saw or heard at any incident.

Without Abraham Zapruder's continued filming of the assassination, the public wouldn't have seen what really happened in the motorcade. There would have been even more unsubstantiated conspiracies written and published without the true facts depicted in the Zapruder film.

Who was Abraham Zapruder? Mr. Zapruder was a Dallas dressmaker with his offices at 501 Elm Street, located across the street from the Texas School Book Depository building.

When Mr. Zapruder left his home on the morning of November 22, 1963, the skies were overcast and threatening. He knew the President of the United States would be passing by his office later that morning but that day seemed poor for picture taking. He left his 8mm movie camera at home.

Just before the President was due to land at Dallas Love Field—the clouds lifted and the sun appeared. Mr. Zapruder decided to head home and get his camera. Returning to his office, he first tried to take pictures from his office window, but he found the camera angle was too narrow. He hurriedly left his office and found a better vantage point in Dealey Plaza. He stood on a four foot concrete pedestal on a slope overlooking Elm Street. To his left stood the Texas School Book Depository building. To his right was the triple underpass; a grassy incline at the top of which stood a wooden fence. He had a perfect vantage point except for a freeway sign on the curb.

Abraham Zapruder wound the camera, set the speed control and tested it—photographing a group of people sitting on cement steps to his left. Looking through the viewfinder, be began to lose his balance and asked his secretary, Marilyn Sitzman, to join him on the pedestal and steady him as he filmed the President's motorcade.

He realized at once what he had captured and rushed to get it developed. Mr. Zapruder sold his historical twenty-six second, 8mm color film of the assassination to *Life* magazine for the sum of $50,000 almost immediately. From those proceeds, Mr. Zapruder donated $25,000 to Marie Tippit for the loss of her husband, J.D. Tippit. With that money, Marie was able to pay off the mortgage on the home she shared with their three children.

Abraham Zapruder died in 1970.

Life returned the film to the Zapruder family and in 1975, *Life* magazine paid an estimated $250,000 to the heirs of the Zapruder family for the film. The film is stored at the National Archives in a twenty-five degree, controlled room at College Park, Maryland.

It is my opinion, gleaned from experience, if an imaginary shooter was hidden behind the wooden fence up the incline of the grassy knoll, Mr. Zapruder would have reacted and distorted the frames of his 8mm film in his camera. The wooden fence was positioned over the left side of Mr. Zapruder, who was standing on a pedestal and was being steadied by his secretary. If a shot was fired from this proximity, his camera would undoubtedly have jerked or flinched. When watching this film there were not any movements of this kind.

Another observation I have found in regard to the grassy knoll, ordinary people do not run toward gunfire. In other depicted film strips you can observe frightened people running up the grassy knoll. Common sense tells a person to run away from gunfire.

In 1998, a team of recognized experts in forensics science were authorized to test all theories of the shooting locations that were theoretically points of origin. They were: Anthony Larry Paul, thirty years ballistics expert; Dr. Vincent Di Maio, Chief Medical Examiner of San Antonio, Texas; Heinz Thummel, laser scientist; Ronald Singer, Chief Criminologist of Tarrant County, Texas; and Robert Groden, photographer expert and conspiracy theorist.

They conducted tests as would the fictional detective, Sherlock Holmes, and eliminated all speculations until the obvious was left. A scientific process in eliminating fringe theories and myths. First, by laser alignment, the grassy knoll was rejected because it was in the incorrect position for any lines of trajectory. Second, a large sign that would have prohibited a shooter from being located in a large portion of the grassy knoll. Third, another location from the grassy knoll in front of the motorcade was rejected because the windshield would have been shattered. Fourth, sewer drainage grate was rejected because there would not have been an opportunity to take an accurate shot. There was sound, laser evidence of perfect alignment of the bullets from the sixth floor of the Texas School Book Depository building to shoot both President Kennedy and Governor John Connally. This is also where the rifle and spent shell casings were found minutes after the shootings.

20

THE PERILS OF PRESIDENTS

IN THE ONE hundred years since 1865, four Presidents of the United States have been assassinated—Abraham Lincoln, James A. Garfield, William McKinley, and John F. Kennedy. During this same period there were three other attacks on the life of a President, a President-elect, and a candidate for the presidency which narrowly failed: Theodore Roosevelt while campaigning in October of 1912; President-elect Franklin Delano Roosevelt, when visiting Miami on February 15, 1933; and President Harry S. Truman on November 1, 1950, when his temporary residence, Blair House, was attacked by Puerto Rican Nationalists. One out of every five presidents since 1865 have been assassinated; there have been attempts on the lives of one out of every three.[27]

In the early days of the republic before the Civil War, there was remarkably little concern about the safety of presidents and few measures were taken to protect them. They were at times the objects of abuse and the recipients of threatening letters as more recent presidents have been, but they did not take the threats seriously and moved freely without protective escorts. On his inauguration day, Thomas Jefferson walked from his boarding house to the Capitol, unaccompanied by any guard, to take the oath of office. There was no police authority in Washington until 1805 when the mayor appointed a high constable and forty deputy constables.

John Quincy Adams received many threatening letters and on one occasion was threatened in person in the White House by a court-martialed army sergeant. In spite of this incident, the President asked for no protection and continued to indulge his fondness for solitary walks and early morning swims in the Potomac. Among pre-Civil War presidents, Andrew Jackson aroused particularly strong feelings. He received many threatening letters which, with a fine contempt, he would endorse and send to the Washington Globe for publication. On one occasion in May 1833, Jackson was assaulted by former Navy Lieutenant Robert B. Randolph, but refused to prosecute him. This was not regarded as an attempted assassination, since Randolph apparently did not intend serious injury.

Less than two years later on the morning of January 10, 1835, as Jackson emerged from the east portico of the Capitol, he was accosted by would-be assassin, Richard Lawrence, an English-born house painter. Lawrence fired his two pistols at the President, but they both misfired. Lawrence was quickly overpowered and held for trial. A jury found him not guilty by reason of insanity. He was confined in jails and mental hospitals for the rest of his life.

The attack on Jackson did not inspire any action to provide protection for the Chief Executive. Jackson's immediate successor, Martin Van Buren, often walked to church alone and rode horseback alone in the woods not far from the White House. In August 1842, after an intoxicated painter had thrown rocks at President John Tyler who was walking the grounds to the south of the White House, Congress passed an act to establish an auxiliary watch for the protection of public and private property in Washington. The force was to consist of a captain and fifteen men. This act was apparently aimed more at the protection of the White House, which had been defaced on occasion, than the president.

Even before he took the oath of office, Abraham Lincoln was thought to be the object of plots and conspiracies to kidnap or kill him. Extremist opponents apparently contemplated desperate measures to prevent his inauguration, and there is some evidence that they plotted to attack him while he was passing through Baltimore on his way to Washington.

For the inauguration, the army took precautions unprecedented at the time and perhaps more elaborate than any precautions since. Soldiers occupied strategic points throughout the city along the procession route and at the Capitol, while armed men in plainclothes mingled with the crowds. Lincoln, in a carriage with President Buchanan, was surrounded on all sides by such dense masses of soldiers that he was almost completely hidden from the view of the crowds. The precautions at the Capitol during the ceremony were almost as thorough and equally successful.

Lincoln lived in peril during all his years in office. The volume of threatening letters remained high throughout the war, but little attention was paid to them. The few letters that were investigated yielded no results. He was reluctant to surround himself with guards and often rejected protection or sought to slip away from it. This has been characteristic of most all American Presidents. They have regarded protection as a necessary affliction at best and contrary to their normal instincts for either personal privacy or freedom to meet the people. In Lincoln these instincts were especially strong, and he suffered with impatience the efforts of his friends, the police, and the military to safeguard him.[28]

In the closing days of the war, rumors of attempts on Lincoln's life persisted. The well-known actor, John Wilkes

Booth, a fanatical Confederate sympathizer, plotted with others for months to kidnap the President. The fall of the Confederacy apparently hardened his determination to kill Lincoln. Booth's opportunity came on Good Friday, April 14, 1865, when he learned that the President would attend a play at Ford's Theater that night. The President's bodyguard for the evening was Patrolman John F. Parker of the Washington Police, a man who proved himself unfit for protective duty. He was supposed to remain on guard in the corridor outside the Presidential box during the entire performance of the play, but soon wandered off to watch the play and then even went outside the theater to have a drink at a nearby saloon. Parker's dereliction of duty left the President totally unprotected. Shortly after 10:00 p.m., Booth found his way up to the Presidential box and shot the President in the head. The President's wound was mortal; he died the next morning, April 15.

A detachment of troops captured Booth on April 26 at a farm near Bowling Green, Virginia; he received a bullet wound and died a few hours later. At a trial in June, a military tribunal sentenced four of Booth's associates to death and four others to terms of imprisonment.[29]

On April 26, 1865, Boston Corbett, a Union Army Sergeant and a member of that troop, disobeyed orders, and shot and killed John Wilkes Booth as he was attempting to surrender. Boston Corbett shot John Wilkes Booth in the neck through an opening in the side wall of the barn. Booth announced that he would fight his way out. The barn was set on fire and as Booth made his way to the door, Corbett shot him. Boston Corbett claimed to have shot Booth because the trapped man was about to shoot one of the officers.[30]

After discharge from the army, Corbett was appointed as the door keeper of the State of Kansas Legislature. Soon after, he became mentally deranged and was placed in a mental hospital, where he eventually died.³¹

Presidents after Lincoln continued to move about Washington virtually unattended, as their predecessors had done before the Civil War, and, as before, such protection as they got at the White House came from the doormen, who were not especially trained for guard duty.

This lack of personal protection for the President again came tragically to the attention of the country with the shooting of President James A. Garfield in 1881. The President's assassin, Charles J. Guiteau, was a self-styled "lawyer, theologian, and politician" who had convinced himself that his unsolicited efforts to help elect Garfield in 1880 entitled him to appointment as a consul in Europe. Bitterly disappointed that the President ignored his repeated written requests for appointment to office and obsessed with a kind of megalomania, he resolved to kill Garfield.³²

Guiteau realized his intent on the morning of July 2, 1881. As Garfield was walking to the train in the Baltimore and Potomac Railroad Station in Washington, Guiteau stepped up and shot him in the back. Garfield did not die from the effects of the wound until September 19, 1881. Although there was evidence of serious abnormality in Guiteau, he was found guilty of murder and sentenced to be hanged. The execution took place on June 30, 1882.³³

There is a story that President Chester A. Arthur, Garfield's successor, once went to a ceremony at the Washington Navy Yard on a public conveyance that he hailed in front of the White House. The President continued to move about Washington, sometimes completely alone, and to travel without special protection.

During Grover Cleveland's second administration (1893-97) the number of threatening letters addressed to the President increased markedly, and Mrs. Cleveland persuaded the President to increase the number of White House policemen to twenty-seven from the three that had constituted the force since the Civil War. In 1894, the Secret Service began to provide protection on an informal basis.[34]

In 1894 while investigating a plot by a group of gamblers in Colorado to assassinate President Cleveland, the Secret Service assigned a small detail of operatives to the White House to help protect him. Secret Service men accompanied the President and his family to their vacation home in Massachusetts; special details protected the President in Washington, on trips, and at special functions. These initially informal and part-time arrangements eventually led to the organization of permanent systematic protection for the President and his family.

During the Spanish-American War the Secret Service stationed a detail at the White House to provide continuous protection for President William McKinley. Between 1894 and 1900, anarchists murdered the President of France, the Premier of Spain, The Empress of Austria, and the King of Italy. At the turn of the century, the Secret Service thought that the strong police action taken against the anarchists in Europe was compelling them to flee and that many were coming to the United States. Concerned about the protection of the President, the Secret Service increased the number of guards and directed that a guard accompany him on all of his trips.

Unlike Lincoln and Garfield, President McKinley was being guarded when he was shot by Leon F. Czolgosz, an American-born twenty-eight-year-old factory worker and farmhand. On September 6, 1901, the President was holding a brief reception for the public in the Temple of Music at the Pan American Exposition in Buffalo. Long lines of people passed between two rows of policemen and soldiers to reach the President and shake his hand. In the immediate vicinity of the President were four Buffalo detectives, four soldiers, and three Secret Service agents. Two of the Secret Service men were facing the President at a distance of three feet. One of them stated later that it was normally his custom to stand at the side of the President on such occasions, but that he had been requested not to do so at this time in order to permit McKinley's secretary and the president of the exposition to stand on either side of McKinley.

Czolgosz joined the line, concealed a pistol under a handkerchief, and when he stood in front of the President, he shot twice through the handkerchief. McKinley fell, critically wounded.

Czolgosz, a self-styled anarchist, did not believe in rulers of any kind. There was evidence that the organized anarchists in the USA did not accept or trust him. He was not admitted as a member to any of the secret anarchist societies. No co-plotters were ever discovered, and there was no evidence that he had confided in anyone. A calm inquiry made by two eminent alienists about a year after Czolgosz was executed found that Czolgosz had been suffering from delusions for some time. One was that he was an anarchist; another was that it was his duty to assassinate the President.

The assassin said he had no grudge against the President personally but did not believe in the republican form of government or in rulers of any kind. In his written confession he included the words, "I don't believe one man should have so much service and another man should have none." As he was strapped to the chair to be electrocuted, he said, "I killed the President because he was the enemy of the good people—the good working people. I am sorry for my crime."

McKinley lingered on for eight days before he died of blood poisoning early in the morning of September 14. Czolgosz, who had been captured immediately, was swiftly tried, convicted, and condemned to death. Although it seemed to some contemporaries that Czolgosz was incompetent, the defense made no effort to plead insanity. Czolgosz was executed forty-five days after the President's death. Investigations by the Buffalo police and the Secret Service revealed no accomplices and no plot of any kind.[35]

Theodore Roosevelt, who had succeeded to the Presidency because of an assassin's bullet, became the object of an assassination attempt a few years after he had left office and when he was no longer under Secret Service protection. During the Presidential campaign of 1912, just as he was about to make a political speech in Milwaukee on October 14, he was shot and wounded in the breast by John N. Schrank, a thirty-six-year-old, German-born ex-tavern keeper. A folded manuscript of his long speech and the metal case for his eyeglasses in the breast pocket of Roosevelt's coat were all that prevented the assassination.

Schrank had had a vision in 1901, induced possibly by McKinley's assassination, which took on meaning for him after Roosevelt, eleven years later, started to campaign for the presidency. In his vision the ghost of McKinley appeared to him and told him not to let a murderer (i.e., Roosevelt, who according to the vision had murdered McKinley) become President. At the bidding of McKinley's ghost, he felt he had no choice but to kill Theodore Roosevelt. After his attempt on Roosevelt, Schrank was found to be insane and was committed to mental hospitals in Wisconsin for the rest of his life.[36]

The attempt on the life of President-elect Franklin D. Roosevelt in 1933 further demonstrated the broad scope and complexity of the protection problems facing the Secret Service. Giuseppe Zangara was a bricklayer and a stonemason with a professed hatred of capitalists and presidents. He seemed to be obsessed with the desire to kill a president. After his arrest, he confessed that he had first planned to go to Washington to kill President Herbert Hoover, but as the cold climate of the North was bad for his stomach trouble, he was loath to leave Miami.

On the night of February 15, 1933 at a political rally in Miami's Bayfront Park, the President-elect sat on the top of the rear seat of his automobile with a small microphone in his hand as he made a short, informal talk. Fortunately for him, however, he slid down into the seat just before Zangara could get near enough to take aim. The assassin's arm may have been jogged just as he shot; the five rounds he directed at Roosevelt went awry. However, he mortally wounded Mayor Anton Cermak of Chicago and hit four other persons; the President-elect, by a miracle, escaped. Zangara, of course, never had any chance of escaping.

Zangara was electrocuted on March 20, 1933, only thirty-three days after his attempt on Roosevelt. No evidence of accomplices or conspiracy came to light, but there was some sensational newspaper speculation, wholly undocumented, that Zangara may have been hired by Chicago gangsters to kill Cermak.[37]

The volume of mail received by the White House had always been large, but it reached huge proportions under Franklin D. Roosevelt. Presidents had always received threatening letters but never in such quantities. To deal with this growing problem, in 1940 the Secret Service established the Protective Research Section to analyze and make available to those charged with protecting the President, information from the White House mail and other sources concerning people potentially capable of committing violence against the President. The Protective Research Section undoubtedly permitted the Secret Service to anticipate and forestall many incidents that might have been embarrassing or harmful to the President.

Although there was no advance warning of the attempt on Harry S. Truman's life on November 1, 1950, the protective measures taken by the Secret Service availed, and the assassins never succeeded in firing directly at the President. The assassins—Oscar Collazo and Griselio Torresola, Puerto Rican Nationalists living in New York—tried to force their way into Blair House, the President's residence while the White House was being repaired. Blair House was guarded by White House policemen and Secret Service agents. In the ensuing gun battle, Torresola and one White House policeman were killed, and Collazo and two White House policemen were wounded. Had the assassins succeeded in entering the front door of Blair House, they would probably have been cut down immediately by another Secret Service agent inside who kept the doorway covered with a submachine gun from his vantage point at the foot of the main stairs. In all, some twenty-seven shots were fired in less than three minutes.

Collazo was brought to trial in 1951 and sentenced to death, but President Truman commuted the sentence to life imprisonment on July 24, 1952. Although there was a great deal of evidence linking Collazo and Torresola to the Nationalist Party of Puerto Rico and its leader, Pedro Albizu Campos, the government could not establish that the attack on the President was part of a larger Nationalist conspiracy.[38]

On September 6, 1975, President Gerald R. Ford was in Sacramento to meet with the Governor of California, Jerry Brown. After breakfast President Ford left the Senator Hotel and walked across the capitol grounds toward the office of Governor Brown.

The weather that morning was clear; the sun was shining brightly, and there were several rows of people standing behind a rope that lined the sidewalk. The crowd was applauding and cheering. President Ford started shaking hands and spotted a woman wearing a bright red dress. She was in the second row, moving right along with the President as if she wanted to shake hands. She thrust her hand under the arms of other spectators and in her hand was a .45-caliber pistol pointed directly at President Ford. The woman yelled, "This country is in a mess. This man is not your President."

Secret Service agent Larry Buendorf reached for the woman's hand and wrestled her to the ground. The other agents grabbed the President and hustled him along the sidewalk into the capitol.

Later President Ford received a full report on the woman who had tried to assassinate him. Her name was Lynette Alice "Squeaky" Fromme, a twenty-fix-year-old disciple of mass killer Charles Manson. On November 26, she was convicted in federal court and was sentenced to spend the rest of her life in prison.

On September 22, 1975, a second attempt to assassinate President Ford happened in San Francisco. At approximately 3:30 p.m., President Ford stepped out of the hotel entrance and walked toward the armored Lincoln Continental limousine. Groups of people stood on both sides of the hotel entrance and there were even larger crowds across the street in Union Square. The President waved at the crowd as he walked toward the limousine.

The sound of a shot rang out. Secret Service agents Jack Merchant and Ron Pontius forced President Ford down behind the car. Then they opened the door and pushed him inside. The agents piled on top of the President and the car took off.

The assailant was a forty-five-year-old woman named Sara Jane Moore, who had ties to radical groups in the San Francisco Bay area. Her weapon was a .38-caliber revolver fired from a distance of forty feet. An alert bystander had noticed the gun in her hand and reached out to deflect her aim. The bullet passed a few feet to the left of President Ford and hit the front of the hotel, then ricocheted off to the right.

Sara Jane Moore was in police custody immediately. Later she pleaded guilty to an attempted murder charge and was sentenced to life imprisonment.[39]

On March 30, 1981, John W. Hinckley, Jr. attempted to assassinate President Ronald Reagan in front of a downtown Washington Hotel. Secret Service agent Dennis McCarthy who was accompanying the President, heard the firecracker pops, dived for the assailant and landed on his back as the last shot was fired. Secret Service agent Jerry Parr instinctively shoved the President inside the car and fell on top of him to protect him. He ordered the driver to proceed directly to the White House while he ran his hands up and down President Reagan's body checking for bullet holes. Finding none he radioed the Secret Service command post at the White House with the first report of the incident.

In pain, President Reagan cursed, "You son-of-a-bitch. You broke my ribs." Agent Jerry Parr saw the President coughing up oxygenated blood.

"Get to George Washington Hospital immediately," Parr barked.[40]

The President had been shot by a troubled man who couldn't distinguish fantasy from reality. It was a movie-driven man who tried to murder our first movie-actor President. John Hinckley was emotionally stunted and had a private life entirely filled with public images—with John Lennon and the Beatles at first. He was drawn to Southern California, arriving in 1976. He did in Hollywood what he had done in Texas and Colorado—went to the movies. That summer he saw *Taxi Driver* fifteen times. He fashioned an imaginary woman he was dating in his letters home describing her as an actress. He told his parents he was going to New York with his friend, but instead went to New Haven to spy on the "real" friend, actress Jodie Foster, who was enrolled at Yale.

Hinckley called and wrote Jodie Foster, saying he would rescue her. He stalked her as the near but unseen suitor. He stalked political figures as a way of purging the world of slobs and rescuing Foster, winning her attention and her love by the same act. Afterward he called his murderous act, "the greatest love offering in the history of the world," one that linked him forever with his beloved in the distant intimacy of shared celebrity. He stated, "I may be in prison and she may be making a movie in Paris or Hollywood, but Jodie and I will always be together, in life and in death."[41]

An earlier televised account had reported that Jim Brady had been killed and that a police officer had been wounded as well in the assassination attempt.

Later it was determined that the bullet that was lodged in Officer Thomas Delahanty's neck was a Devastator bullet, meaning it contained a small explosive charge that could have killed him instantly. Devastator bullets are designed to kill people, though the manufacturers insist they are for hunting. Once discharged, it explodes on contact, sending the fragments through wherever the bullet hit. Fortunately for the police officer, the bullet was removed before it could cause any further damage. Unfortunately for Jim Brady, the bullet he took in the head exploded in his brain before it could be removed.[42]

President Reagan recovered from his chest wound. The quick decision by Secret Service agent Jerry Parr to take him to the hospital saved his life.

Fifteen months later, at the end of a seven week trial, a federal jury found John W. Hinckley, Jr. not guilty by reason of insanity. A judge committed him to St. Elizabeth Hospital, a mental institution in Washington, D.C.[43]

Frank Eugene Corder seemed to know exactly how he wanted to die. Sometime before midnight on September 11, 1994, he stole a single-engine plane from the airport north of Baltimore and headed to Washington, D.C. He came in low over the White House south lawn, clipped a hedge, skidded across the green lawn that girds the south portico and crashed into a wall two stories below the Presidential bedroom. Corder was killed on impact.

President Bill Clinton and the First Family had fortunately been spending the night across Pennsylvania Avenue at Blair House while White House workers repaired faulty duct work.

Corder, a man who had recently suffered multiple losses in his life including his business; his father, who had died in 1995; and his marriage, had talked of suicide. Corder said he believed crashing an airplane into the White House would be a novel way to die.

At 2:00 a.m. on that Monday, Corder's low-flying, small Cessna gave White House security personnel just enough time to dive out of the way. The unlikely incident confirmed publicly what security officials had long feared in private: the White House was vulnerable to sneak attack from the air.[44]

On October 29, 1994, a brooding Colorado Springs upholsterer, Francisco Martin Duran, a twenty-six-year-old pulled a Chinese-made SKS semiautomatic assault rifle from under his coat and shot twenty-seven rounds of ammunition in short bursts across the north side of the building. Five bullets pocked the White House mansion's four-foot-thick sandstone wall, and three shattered a window and chipped the stone of the press briefing room near the west wing. Several bullets burrowed into trees. President Clinton, who was inside the White House watching a football game, was probably the safest person in the area, given the bulletproof glass and scores of Secret Service officers between him and the gunman.

The accused gunman, Duran, ran along the White House fence firing at the building. When he tried to reload his weapon, a tourist, thirty-four-year-old Harry Rakosky, who worked security in Texas, tackled the gunman and held him for the Secret Service. U.S. prosecutors charged him with attempted assassination, based on the notes and other material found in his nearby pickup truck and threatening remarks he allegedly made to a co-worker at the Colorado Springs Broadmoor Hotel.[45]

21

PROTECTING THE PRESIDENT

THE ASSASSINATION OF President Kennedy was a cruel and shocking act of violence directed against a man, a family, a nation, and against all mankind. A young and vigorous leader whose years of public and private life stretched before him, he was the victim of the fourth presidential assassination in the history of a country dedicated to the concepts of reasoned argument and peaceful political change.[46]

President John F. Kennedy's automobile was a specially designed 1961 Lincoln convertible with two collapsible jump seats between the front and rear seats. It was outfitted with a clear plastic bubbletop, which was neither bulletproof nor bullet resistant.

Early in the morning light rain was falling in Dallas, but it stopped just as quickly as it started. The skies became a bright blue with a few scattered, puffy white clouds. It was going to be a beautiful day. Because the skies had cleared in Dallas, Secret Service Special Agent Winston G. Lawson directed that the top not be used for the day's activities. Agent Lawson acted on instructions he had received earlier from Assistant Special Agent in Charge Roy H. Kellerman. Agent Kellerman had discussed the matter of the "bubbletop" with Kenneth

O'Donnell, special assistant to the President, whose instructions were, "If the weather is clear and it is not raining, have the bubbletop off."

President Kennedy liked outdoor appearances because more people could see and hear him. Before leaving the hotel in Fort Worth, President Kennedy, Mrs. Kennedy and Kenneth O'Donnell talked about the risks inherent in presidential public appearances.

Arriving at Love Field at 11:40 a.m. and after a welcome from the Dallas reception committee, President Kennedy and Mrs. Kennedy walked along a chain link fence at the reception area greeting a large crowd of spectators that had gathered behind the fence. Secret Service agents formed a cordon to keep the press and photographers from impeding their passage and scanned the crowd for threatening movements. Dallas police stood at intervals along the fence and Dallas plainclothesmen mixed in the crowd. Vice President and Mrs. Johnson followed along the fence, guarded by four members of the Vice President detail. Approximately ten minutes after arrival at Love Field, the President and Mrs. Kennedy went to the presidential automobile to begin the motorcade through downtown Dallas.

President Kennedy rode on the right-hand side of the rear seat with Mrs. Kennedy on his left. Governor Connally occupied the right jump seat, Mrs. Connally the left jump seat. Driving the presidential limousine was Secret Service Special Agent William R. Greer. On his right sat Assistant Special Agent in Charge Roy H. Kellerman. Kellerman's responsibilities included maintaining radio communications with the lead and follow-up cars, scanning the route, and getting out and standing near the President when the car stopped.

Four motorcycle Dallas police officers, two on each side, flanked the rear of the presidential car. They were to provide some cover for the President, but their main purpose was to keep back the crowd. On previous occasions, the President had requested that, to the extent possible, the flanking motorcycles keep back from the sides of his car.

The follow-up car was an eight passenger 1955 Cadillac convertible outfitted for the Secret Service that followed closely behind the President's car. It carried eight Secret Service agents—two in the front seat, two in the rear, and two on each of the right and left running boards. Each agent carried a .38 caliber pistol, and a shotgun and automatic rifle were also available. Presidential assistant David F. Powers and Kenneth O'Donnell sat in the right and left jump seats, respectively.

The agents in the car, under established procedure, had instructions to watch the route for signs of trouble, scanning not only the crowds but the windows and roofs of buildings, overpasses, and crossings. They were instructed to watch particularly for thrown objects, sudden actions in the crowd, and any movement toward the presidential car.

The motorcade left Love Field shortly after 11:50 a.m. and drove at speeds up to twenty-five to thirty miles an hour through thinly populated areas on the outskirts of downtown Dallas. At the President's direction, his automobile stopped twice, the first time to permit him to respond to a sign asking him to shake hands. During this brief stop, agents in the front positions on the running boards of the presidential follow-up car came forward and stood beside the President's car, looking out toward the crowd, and Special Agent Kellerman assumed his position next to the car. On the other occasion, the President halted the motorcade to speak to a Catholic nun and a group of small children.

In the downtown area, large crowds of spectators gave the President a tremendous reception. The crowds were so dense that Special Agent Clinton J. Hill had to leave the left front running board of the President's follow-up car four times to ride the rear of the President's limousine. Several times Special Agent John D. Ready came forward from the right front running board of the Presidential follow-up car to the right side of the President's car. Special Agent Glen A. Bennett once left his place inside the follow-up car to help keep the crowd away from the President's car. When a teenage boy ran toward the rear of the President's car, Ready left the running board to chase the boy back into the crowd. On several occasions when the Vice President's car was slowed down by the throng, Special Agent Rufus W. Youngblood stepped out to hold the crowd back.

According to plan, the President's motorcade proceeded west through downtown Dallas on Main Street to the intersection of Houston Street, which marks the beginning of Dealey Plaza. From Main Street the motorcade turned right and went north on Houston Street, passing tall buildings on the right, and headed toward the Texas School Book Depository building. The spectators were thickly congregated in front of the building which lined the east side of Houston Street, but the crowd thinned abruptly along Elm Street, which curves in a southwest direction as it proceeds toward the triple underpass on the Stemmons Freeway.

As the motorcade approached the intersection of Houston and Elm Streets, there was general gratification in the Presidential party about the enthusiastic reception. Evaluating the political overtones, Kenneth O'Donnell was especially pleased because it convinced him that the average Dallas resident was like other American citizens in respecting and admiring the President. Mrs. Connally, elated by the reception turned to President Kennedy and said, "Mr. President, you can't say Dallas doesn't love you." The President replied, "That is very obvious."

At 12:30 p.m., c.s.t. [sic], as the President's open limousine proceeded at approximately eleven miles per hour along Elm Street toward the triple underpass, shots fired from a rifle that mortally wounded President Kennedy and seriously injured Governor John Connally.[47]

22

AWARDS AND HONORS

I RECEIVED MANY letters throughout our nation, congratulating me for bravery and requests for autographs. It was a wonderful feeling to know that I was being recognized.

Lloyd Shearer, a writer for *Parade Magazine*, came to Dallas and wrote an outstanding article on the capture of Oswald which included the mentioning of my family and our simple lifestyle. Congressman Joe Pool of Dallas submitted this same article before the 88th Congress and they were in mutual accord with the Honorable Joe Pool to place it and make it part of the official Congressional Record, 2nd Session, March 18, 1964, pages A1401 and A1402, of the Appendix. It honored me greatly to know that our nation's leaders and lawmakers wanted me to have this national recognition for my deeds that day in Dallas.

In April of 1964, the first honor and recognition to me was by the Colorado Police Protective Association. My wife, Sally, and I were invited to Pueblo, Colorado to attend their annual meeting and convention.

Arriving at the airport in Denver, we were met by a host of police officers, city and state officials, and members of the news media. Sally was presented a bouquet of beautiful red roses. The chief of police of Denver placed their city's symbol, a silver dollar, around my neck. Letters denoting the official welcome to the great state of Colorado and the city of Denver were presented to us from representatives of the mayor of Denver and the governor of Colorado.

We were overwhelmed by the warm reception and were ushered to the celebrity room of the airport for a press conference. A barrage of questions about the assassination and the arrest of Oswald were thrown at us from all sides by representatives of the news media.

After the lights of the television cameras had faded, we were led to a waiting limousine; an extended motorcade was formed and we were chauffeured to Colorado Springs for a brief stop to tour their new police station. While there, a group of Scouts that were touring, had learned who I was, and immediately had surrounded me and were pressing for autographs. I felt like a rock star with all of the attention I was getting from these young, eager boys and girls. It was one of my greatest thrills.

Then we continued on to Pueblo. Our motorcade was escorted by the chief of the highway patrol of Colorado. On our arrival at Pueblo, we were shown to our suite of rooms which were filled with flowers, candy, and a huge basket of fresh fruit. The red carpet and royal treatment was being experienced by us first hand. It was elegant and exciting to say the least.

During the convention, we had the pleasure of meeting and talking with many state dignitaries and officials.

At the banquet, I was presented with a beautifully inscribed plaque. They also presented a gold key to the city of Pueblo. The wives auxiliary of the association presented Sally with a beautiful engraved silver tray.

At the eighteenth annual Dallas police awards dinner on April 23, 1964, Police Chief Jesse E. Curry presented me with the city's highest award, the Dallas Police Medal of Honor. The Citizens Traffic Commission of Dallas presented the Award of Honor plaque. I personally felt that the greatest honor was bestowed when my own police department awarded me their highest medal, The Medal of Honor.

On May 2, 1964, Sally and I were invited to Chicago to be honored by the National Police Officers Association of America. The red carpet was once again rolled out for us. They too provided us with a limousine and a beautiful suite of rooms.

We dined at the famous Fanny's restaurant in Evanston and attended the critically acclaimed Broadway play, *How to Succeed in Business Without Really Trying*. This was really a first for both of us. We had never experienced a live production before. After the theatre we were royally wined and dined at the celebrated Pump Room, the "in place" of Chicago where we enjoyed meeting and talking to some very distinguished people—an unforgettable evening filled with many pleasurable memories.

The following night, the awards dinner was held at Hugh Hefner's famous Playboy Club, where Hugh Hefner presented me with a life-time membership to all the Playboy Clubs. I was presented a beautiful plaque from the National Police Officers Association of America with the Medal of Valor attached. I was then informed me that my name and picture would be placed in the Police Hall of Fame at Venice, Florida. It was eventually moved to Miami, Florida.

During our visit, we were afforded the opportunity to meet and make many new friends. I made an appearance at one of the local television stations and as we were waiting to go on the air, Governor George Wallace of Alabama and his wife Lurleen came out of the studio, and we were introduced to them. At that particular time, Governor Wallace was running for President. It was very interesting to talk with the Governor and listen to his ideas. Of course, he was just as equally interested in meeting me.

We also toured the famous Marshall Field's department store and were treated to lunch and a fashion show. The people of Chicago left a lasting impression of warmth and friendliness that shall never be forgotten.

On our return to Dallas, we were extended a cordial invitation from the fabulous Hotel Fontainebleau in Miami Beach, Florida to be their guests for a family vacation that included our two daughters, Vicki and Michelle. We enjoyed a pleasant, relaxing time, taking full advantage of the beautiful beaches and the glorious Miami sun. I was presented the tiny key to Miami Beach. I must agree with the philosophy, "The Smaller the Key, The Larger the City's Heart."

Every day we were in the Miami area I was interviewed by newspaper reporters and television stations. I was interviewed at midnight on *The Larry King Radio Talk Show* at the Surfside Six Studio, a houseboat that was tied up on the inland waterway, across from the Hotel Fontainebleau. What a great experience that was! Larry King was a great radio talk show host and was very knowledgeable and current on the subject matter. I liked him immediately and he was very pleasant to be around.

On our return to Dallas we made a brief stop to visit the Police Hall of Fame in Venice, Florida. This memorial, dedicated to police officers throughout our nation, is a living memorial which should be seen by everyone. It offers a better understanding of who and what the police officer is to his community. The director, Gerald Arenberg, gave us a guided tour of the museum and I was introduced to a touring group of teachers and school children. They were all interested and curious and wanted to know all about the arrest and capture of Oswald. I was flattered and thrilled that they had an interest in me and the part that I played on that day in Dallas.

In October we were invited again to be honored. This time our travels took us to Boston to be honored by The 100 Club of Massachusetts. This organization was formed to benefit the widows and orphans of slain police officers and firemen. Their objectives are to pay any debts or obligations left by those killed while performing their duties.

At the awards dinner, I was pleasantly surprised with a check of $1,000, but I could not personally accept the check. So, they made the check out to my wife, Sally. If I had accepted the money, I would have been obligated to donate it to the Police and Fire Pension Fund in Dallas. However, I was able to accept a handsome gold wristwatch which was beautifully inscribed.

Again we were afforded the opportunity to meet and make many wonderful new friends at the dinner. I knew that I was facing many close and dear friends of the late President John F. Kennedy. As I addressed the crowd, I expressed my sorrow to them that I was in Boston under such tragic circumstances. Police Commissioner Edmund L. McNamara made me an Honorary Commissioner of the Boston Police; Sheriff Howard W. Fitzpatrick deputized me as an Honorary Deputy Sheriff of Middlesex County; Mr. George Swartz, President of The 100 Club of Massachusetts, awarded me an Honorary membership to The 100 Clubs founded by Mr. William Packer of Detroit, Michigan.

George Swartz had stated their organization was the first to contribute to Marie Tippit, widow of Officer J.D. Tippit, sending her a check for $500 on the night of November 22, 1963.

George Swartz invited my family and me to be his guests at his Cape Cod home in Falmouth whenever we came back in New England to visit my mother in Maine. I accepted his invitation and told him we had planned a trip to Maine next summer and we would make plans to return to Dallas by way of Cape Cod.

During my twenty-five years with the Dallas Police Department, I was awarded many honors, including:

- Twenty-six letters of Commendations
- Police Officer Of The Year, 1960
- Life Saving Award
- Dallas Police Medal of Honor
- City of Dallas Award of Honor
- Elected to the National Police Hall of Fame and Awarded the Medal of Valor by The National Police Officers of America
- The Colorado Police Protective Association Award of Honor
- The Police Sergeant's Association, an Honorary Chicago Police Sergeant
- The 100 Club of Boston, honored for Outstanding Performance for the Arrest and Capture of Lee Harvey Oswald
- Keys to the cities of Pueblo, Colorado; Miami Beach, Florida
- Key to the Chicago Playboy Club
- Featured in *Life* magazine November 1983
- Television series "Top Cops," 1990

To continue awards and honors, I have received invitations to speak at school classes from sixth graders up to college students over the years. I was always eager to speak to students and adults alike and give them the true facts of President Kennedy's assassination, and the capture and arrest of Lee Harvey Oswald. Mainly because of all the half-truths and outright lies told by conspiracy theorists.

I was there and a witness to the factual evidences that were developed by basic police revelations, unbiased with documented facts. The factual, true evidence cannot be anything but the whole truth. I have been invited to be a guest speaker by Homicide Conference Enforcement personnel over the country. These groups represent police officers from all over the United States of America. These included conferences in Kansas City, Missouri during 2000 and 2002 as well as the Dover, Delaware conference in 2001 and 2002.

In October 2003, I was again the guest speaker in Branson, Missouri for a group of law enforcement officers that represented the Western District of U.S. Attorneys. In November 2003, I was also invited to Branson, Missouri to attend the United States of America Congressional Medal of Honor recipient's formal banquet. I was introduced to the audience as the Medal of Honor recipient of the Dallas police.

Ten days later, I was invited back to Branson to attend the benefit for The National Cemetery at Arlington, Virginia. Also, Ross Perot received the Humanitarian Award. Again, I was introduced to the audience, as the man that arrested accused assassin, Lee Harvey Oswald of President John F. Kennedy. I met very important dignitaries that attended including Mr. Perot.

In May 2004, we were invited to South Plainfield, New Jersey. I was the guest speaker at South Plainfield High School to the students and the public of South Plainfield, New Jersey.

We were received with much love and kindness by everyone. We toured the New Jersey state police headquarters and museum. The following day we visited the Statue of Liberty and New York City, which included Times Square and Ground Zero. We paused to pray for all the people that didn't make it and for those left behind that still grieve daily. We also toured the United Nations, Broadway and 42nd Street, and most of Manhattan. We went through the tunnel to Hoboken for lunch.

Afterward, we hurried back to South Plainfield for a high school baseball game and I was given the honor to throw out the first baseball. After my speech that night in the school auditorium, I was awarded a total of five plaques from South Plainfield: the high school, the police department, the Mayor, the citizens of South Plainfield and the state of New Jersey Assemblymen, Joint Legislative Resolution. I was grateful, humbled and proud.

23

ROCKY MARCIANO

ONE SPRING DAY in 1969, George Swartz, my friend and confidant from Boston, called and told me that he was Rocky Marciano's business advisor and that Rocky was going to be in Dallas the next day. George continued by saying, "Rocky told me that he would like to meet you while he's in Dallas."

Almost speechless, I replied, "George, that would be one of the greatest thrills of my life. I could never imagine this ever happening to me!"

"I gave Rocky your telephone number and he'll call you from Houston and let you know when he gets in Dallas. Rocky will be staying at the Sheraton Hotel in downtown Dallas."

"George, that will be just great. You know that Rocky is one of my biggest idols and that I have admired him for years. I can't believe I will actually meet the great Rocky Marciano. I'd like to make arrangements to take him out for dinner at one of Dallas' finest Italian restaurants."

"Okay, Nick. Let me know how things work out."

"Thanks, George. I'll be waiting for his call. I'll be talking to you soon and thanks again."

Hanging up the phone, goose bumps popped up on my arms and the fine hairs on my neck bristled. What an honor! I knew that Rocky was Italian and I thought of an Italian restaurant, the Egyptian Lounge on Mockingbird Lane, owned and operated by the Campisi brothers, Joe and Sam. Leave it to Texans to name an Italian restaurant something completely different and unrelated to an Italian name. On the restaurant wall was a life-size poster of Rocky Marciano in his fighting stance and they had expressed their admiration for the great Rocky Marciano.

As plainclothes detectives, my partner Gene Johnston and I had dinner at this popular Italian restaurant occasionally and the food was outstanding. On the weekend there were long lines outside extending onto the sidewalk.

I remember one Friday evening, Gene and I entered the back door to the restaurant to avoid the standing lines out front. The rear door was near the office and the office door was slightly ajar, and we could overhear what appeared to be the termination of a telephone conversation. When we walked inside the office, Papa Campisi was leaning back watching a flickering black and white TV and Joe Campisi was just hanging up the phone and greeted us with a smile. He said, "How would you guys like to get in on a hot horse in New Orleans at the fairgrounds? I just got off the phone talking to Marcello and he owns a hot horse running tomorrow and it's a sure thing, if you know what I mean!"

Of course, Gene and I immediately knew who Carlos Marcello was. He was the "Mafia" boss of the "Dixie Mafia" and was well known throughout the South and Southwest by all police agencies. Jokingly, with tongue-in-cheek, I replied, "Yeah, do you know any bookies?"

Knowing full well he knew what I meant, Joe answered with a weak smile, "Why, you boys know I don't know anything about bookies or gamblin' unless I'm at the track!"

Quickly changing the subject, he said, "I'll bet you guys are hungry. Sam, find these fellows a good table."

We followed Sam into a private dining room and had our dinner. On leaving, we asked for the check but Sam refused so we left a ten dollar tip for the waitress. That made us both feel better about the incident that took place in their private office. When I called and told Sam Campisi about Rocky Marciano, he was so excited the telephone fell from his hand and I could hear it bang to the floor.

Sam recovered and said, "We would be honored to serve the great Rocky Marciano! What time do you want us to set it up?"

"After I meet and check with Rocky tomorrow, I will call and give you a time."

Early the next morning I was up, shaved, showered and dressed in my Sunday best gray suit. The day before I had arranged to be off by using some of my accumulated "comp time." Promptly at 10:00 a.m. the phone rang. With nervous anticipation, I picked up the receiver and spoke in a clear voice, "Hello, this is Nick McDonald!"

"This is Rocky Marciano, Nick."

"Hi, Mr. Marciano. Thank you for calling; George Swartz said you'd call. I'm really anxious to meet you!"

"First of all, Nick, my name is Rocky. My father is Mr. Marciano, okay? Okay! I'm checked in at the Sheraton in room 2400. When can you come up? I'm anxious to meet you, too! George has told me all about you."

"Well, Mr. Marciano—I mean Rocky, I'm on my way and will be there in about thirty minutes. I am really looking forward to meeting you."

I went up the express elevator to Rocky's room and knocked on his suite. His traveling press agent, Sam, answered the door and invited me in. As I entered the spacious rooms,

Rocky was coming out of the bedroom buttoning a draped, white shirt over his expansive chest, stretching the seams of a white undershirt. A damp, ringlet of his jet black hair lingered carelessly on his brow. He was in such great physical shape it looked as if he was ready to enter the ring for another challenge at any time.

He extended a massive hand to me and his grip was unbelievable. My hand seemed to disappear into his huge, solid hand. The mighty right hand that had put his opponents on the canvas many, many times.

Rocky said, "Hi, Nick. I'm glad to meet you. I just finished exercising and got a quick shower."

"Thanks, Rocky. The pleasure is all mine, believe me. How in the world do you keep in such great shape and maintain your physical strength?"

"As a matter of fact," he answered, "I try to run every day no matter where I am. This morning I ran down the hotel stairwell to the lobby, and then I ran back up to my room."

I said, "Man, you must be exhausted!"

He said, "No, no. I'm ready to eat Italian!"

He playfully jabbed my right shoulder with his left arm, almost knocking me down. I said with a grin, rubbing my shoulder, "Rocky, if that was your sample of playing, I feel sorry for all those men that were on the receiving end of your serious jabs and right crosses. No wonder you're the undefeated heavyweight champion of the world!"

I called Sam Campisi and told him we were on the way and he was thrilled. We went in my personal car and Rocky understood since I was a police officer, I would be his personal bodyguard, if need be.

When we arrived at the Egyptian Lounge, Sam met us at the door and ushered us into their very private dining room. Sam had even moved Rocky's life-size poster from the main dining room to this room, with a bright, overhead spotlight directed onto it.

This small but adequate dining room was filled with a few members of the Campisi family and their close friends. They all wanted to meet their boxing hero. One by one they came up and Rocky graciously took each of their extended hands, even though some of them may have been "black hands" of the "Mafia." After greeting Rocky, everyone left except for the Campisi family. Sam came over to Rocky and asked if he would please autograph his poster. Without hesitation and the gentleman that he was, Rocky took Sam's pen and scrawled his signature on the poster.

We sat down at the checkered cloth table with the ever present Chianti wine bottle with melted was candle. Waitresses began to bring trays containing all types of steaming Italian pasta dishes. Sam said, "Rocky, I didn't know if you had a favorite dish, so we made all of our popular dishes for you to choose or eat from each dish, if you wish."

Rocky smiled and said, "I love each and every one of them; thank you so much, Sam!"

Rosé wine and garlic bread were served with the Italian dishes. We devoured all the food we could possibly hold or ever could hope to hold. It was delicious! After dining, Rocky shook hands all around, including the waitresses and even went in the kitchen to thank the chef and his staff. Sam followed us out to the car and couldn't thank Rocky enough for making a special visit to their restaurant and giving him the opportunity to meet the one and only Rocky Marciano.

After saying our goodbyes, and on the return trip to the hotel, Rocky said to me, "Okay, Nick, enough about me. I want to hear all about your capture and arrest of that son-of-a-bitch assassin, Oswald!"

I took Rocky step-by-step through that whole tragic day. When I was finished with my personal account, Rocky leaned back against the passenger seat and gave a deflated sigh of relief. It was as if he was right beside me during the whole ordeal, and he, himself, had fought the fight.

Rocky said, "Nick, you are a champ in your own right and it has been my pleasure in meeting and being with you throughout this whole enjoyable day. I can't thank you enough for being the hero that you are. Before we part, I want you to take that basket of fruit the hotel left in my suite to your children. I never eat the stuff anyway."

"Thank you, Rocky. The girls will be thrilled to know you sent this basket of fruit to them."

Saying our farewells, I left with a happy, full feeling of meeting and knowing a real gentleman. Little did I know that I would never see him again. On August 31, 1969, near Newton, Iowa, the small light plane that Rocky was using on his tour suddenly crashed and Rocky Marciano was killed instantly.

When I heard this terrible news, I was devastated. I had lost another dear friend to tragedy. President John F. Kennedy, Officer J.D. Tippit, Robert F. Kennedy, Reverend Martin Luther King, Jr. and now Rocky Marciano, my new friend and champion.

The nation mourned along with Rocky's many friends and relatives. He had touched many lives and every one was better from having known this great man and champion; the people's champion. Goodbye, Rocky Marciano. Believe me, it was my pleasure.

24

HYANNIS PORT

IN THE SUMMER of 1965 we made our return trip back to Dallas and went by way of Cape Cod as we had promised. The Swartz's arranged a reception for us at their beautiful Cape Cod home by the sea. There were a couple of newspaper reporters and a house full of people that were friends and neighbors of the Kennedy family, including Chief of Police Hinckley of Hyannis Port.

One of the reporters cornered me and started interviewing me. During the interview, he stopped and was staring into my eyes and said, "It seems to me that you were the only one that did anything right that day in Dallas!"

With a shrug of my shoulders I said, "Thanks, you're probably right!"

Walking away from the inquiring reporter, I went over to Chief Hinckley and he began telling me that he had been a close friend to the Kennedy family for many years and on the night Jack Kennedy was elected President, he had given him a tie clasp which depicted "P-T boat 109" with the words "Kennedy-60" engraved on the hull.

Chief Hinckley then took this tie clasp from his tie and placed it on mine. I tried to refuse this honored gesture, but he expressed his desire for me to keep it in remembrance of Jack Kennedy. He extended an invitation for us to visit the town of Hyannis Port and possibly tour the Kennedy compound.

The next day following the reception at the Swartz's home, George took us by ferry to Martha's Vineyard for a tour of the island. The affluence and vast wealth of the Vineyard community can only be compared to Newport and Palm Beach. The village, Oak Bluffs, was a quiet, quaint little hamlet, nestled on Nantucket Sound, very private and protected. We were met at the ferry landing by Sergeant Robert T. Cannon, Commander of the Oak Bluffs State Police Barracks. He was very cordial and accommodating. We were introduced to the Vineyard, Dukes County, and state law enforcement officials, including Mr. Al Brickman, a local businessman that was sponsoring a chapter of The 100 Club on the island. After a brief tour of the unrestricted areas of residential properties and retail outlets, we were wined and dined at a local eatery.

Everything considered, it was a very pleasant, informative, one-day visit to the Vineyard. The welcoming attitude and friendliness extended to me and my family can only be compared to southern hospitality in the nicest way possible.

The following afternoon, Mr. and Mrs. Swartz took us to Hyannis Port from their home in Falmouth. We were greeted at the Hyannis Port Police Station by Sergeant Coughlin. Chief Hinckley had arranged for him to be our personal guide. He was very courteous as well as efficient, making sure that we had the opportunity of seeing everything connected with the Kennedy family. The view from the compound of Nantucket Sound, and the vast Atlantic Ocean was unblemished. There were sailboats of every description with their pure white and brightly colored sails billowing and catching each breath of the wind.

The Kennedy compound itself was protected by a security of local police officers to discourage tourists from approaching. We were permitted to enter by the consent of the Secret Service agents assigned to the protection of Mrs. Jacqueline Kennedy, Caroline and John-John.

Very quietly and discreetly, we passed through the ten foot stockade fence that completely surrounded the John F. Kennedy home. A Secret Service agent was kind enough to point out the late President Kennedy's bedroom, located on the second floor of the spacious home. As I looked up at the window, I could see Jackie Kennedy moving about the room.

Thoughts came to me of the life she and her husband shared in their short, but productive lives together. Jackie first met Jack Kennedy, the Congressman, at a dinner party in 1951. In June 1953 they became engaged and three months later they were married. John F. Kennedy was elected President in 1960, and Jackie became our First Lady.

She was an enchanting, young wife in the White House. Style was her thing. Fashionable and attractive, ever mindful of her image. In public, she rarely faltered. This was a lady who in a single year had endured the loss of an infant son and then the assassination of her husband three months later. I remember the image of her marching behind her husband's horse-drawn funeral caisson. She had won a world's admiration for her dignity at this time of grieving. She gave the impression she could suffer the greatest of difficulties with grace. Her bravery and dignity touched the hearts, not only of the American people, but the hearts of people all over the world. Her strength and composure helped make the pain of death more acceptable in the loss of our young President.

Now a single mother raising her children in privacy, she knew how to be a mother to her children and a fierce protector of her family. She wanted to live a life without publicity, ever quiet, ever insulating her children and her thoughts from public scrutiny. She often hid behind sunglasses and kerchiefs, but everything called attention. Her wealth, her dark wide-eyed beauty and social birth, and to have been the First Lady of our nation.

As we stood on this historic site, I felt we were invading their privacy by this intrusion and suggested to my family that we should leave quietly. We left and our guide took us on an impromptu tour, showing us the homes in which various members of the Kennedy family resided.

As we were leaving the protected area, we saw Caroline riding her bicycle up a deserted street behind the compound. A Secret Service agent, who was riding another bicycle, met Caroline at the corner and asked where she was going. Very cheerfully she replied, "I am trying to get away and hide from him!" (Meaning the other agent.)

As the agent accompanied her through the closing gates of the compound, another agent came running up the deserted street and was frantically trying to talk into his walkie-talkie. Breathlessly, he ran up to our police car and asked if we had seen Caroline. We told him that the other agent had caught up with her and had taken her into the compound.

He gave a great sigh of relief and said, "The children were trying to get away and hide from me."

My children were laughing playfully at Caroline's antics of disrupting the Secret Service agent in their game of hide-and-seek. As adults, we were saddened with the thought that there was a possibility harm could come to those innocent, little children.

A memorable but saddening experience was our visit to the chapel where the Kennedys worshipped. As we entered, I could feel the presence of God all around. I walked slowly and quietly to the pew that was designated with a plaque inscribed, "In Memory of President John F. Kennedy."

I was told this was the pew he had occupied when he had worshipped. I gently placed my hand on the smooth, fine-grained wood of the now empty pew where our late and great President had often prayed. Bowing my head, I said a silent prayer as I blinked the tears from my eyes, trying to discourage my choking emotions.

I turned Sally's hand, and with our children Vicki and Michelle, walked silently from the chapel... Remembering what a senseless loss our nation, for that matter the world, had suffered when President Kennedy was murdered by a hateful bullet from an assassin's rifle.

25

ROSE DAISY AND I

IN THE EARLY 1970s, Sally and I took a vacation to Hot Springs, Arkansas and fell in love with the area. I was born and raised in Arkansas, and I remembered the beauty of Hot Springs. We loved the quaint tourist town with its thermal baths, the unbelievable tree-lined mountains, and the many clear blue lakes meandering through the valley of the vapors. Not to mention entertainment of all kinds—dining establishments, nightclubs, thoroughbred horse racing, water sports, great fishing, and sport hunting in the surrounding woods.

With retirement not too far in our future, we begin to look at the available real estate in the lake area. After careful consideration, we found a cute little condo on Lake Hamilton in a great location within five minutes of shopping. It was our vacation retirement dream.

In 1973, Sally started to develop health problems. She was in and out of the hospital for the next three years. In 1976, she had a massive stroke and never recovered. She passed away March 16, 1976. We were married for twenty-five wonderful years, and blessed with two beautiful daughters. She was only forty-four-years-old.

From 1977 to 1980, I was a supervisor of the Dallas Police Communications Division, supervising the Police Radio Dispatchers and the 911 Emergency Telephone Operators.

This was one of my most challenging assignments; trying to keep twenty-six females efficient, and happy in the workplace was almost an impossible task, especially with all the stress-related calls for police assistance they handled day in and day out. I had no major problems with the police officers because they were sworn personnel and were aware that insubordination could result in serious charges and they could be terminated. On the other hand, telephone clerks were all civilians, and came under a different set of rules and regulations.

After losing my wife, I was single and alone. I tried to play the rat race single's game, and found it was not for me. I'd been married twenty-five years, and I was forty-nine-years-old, and balding.

It was December 1977. My two daughters were married and had lives of their own, and I wasn't getting any younger. I was anxious to find someone to share my life.

During a shift two days before Christmas Eve, one of my single telephone clerks, Rose Daisy Brown, a beautiful blonde lady, passed a handwritten note to me. The note read: *Xmas Eve at my girlfriend's house for drinks. What do you say?*

I picked up the phone, dialed her extension and said, "Christmas Eve is two days away; why don't we go out for dinner tonight. We can get to know each other a little better before being with a bunch of other people, okay?"

She answered, "That's a good idea. Pick me up around seven. Do you know where I live?"

"Of course I do. I have all your information right here!" This was the beautiful beginning of our relationship.

From that day on, we got along famously and fell in love without even planning on it. It just happened! We were seeing each other daily at work and dating every night. Over the New Year's holiday, and the beginning of 1978, I went to Hot Springs to finish up a few little odd jobs in the condominium. I was trying to make myself busy, and not think about my blonde Rosie back in Dallas. I missed her terribly, and I knew then I had fallen deeply in love. I had not told her I loved her because I was afraid she didn't love me as I loved her. I couldn't stand it any longer.

I called her long distance. I told her how much I missed her, wanted to be with her, and that I loved her very much.

Rosie said, "I miss you, and I love you, too! I was afraid to say it before, because I wanted you to love me, too!"

We were married April 22, 1978. After we were married, we learned it was policy that a husband and wife could not work together on the same shift within the police department. Especially a supervisor and an employee.

Rosie returned to the midnight shift. When she got off work, I was going on duty. She slept during the day while I worked. When I got home she was up and awake. Then we had time together until 10:00 p.m. She went to work, and I went to bed. This lasted two more years, and we both retired July 29, 1980. We loaded up our stuff in a U-Haul, and left for Hot Springs. Just as I planned many years before—and returned to my home state.

I knew Rosie might have a difficult time adjusting to retirement in another home and another state. Rosie was born in Dallas and Texas was her state. All of her family and friends were in Texas, but I reassured her we could always go back for visits. With her love for adventure and her quest to explore new beginnings and try new things, I was confident she would make the best of it—and she did!

After we had settled in, Rosie wanted to return to her art work of sketching and oil painting to fill her days. She decided to take refresher courses in art offered by the local YMCA. She had only been in class for two weeks when the other art students commented that Rosie had a natural talent. She demonstrated she knew more about art than others in her class.

It wasn't long before she was noticed and was winning blue ribbons at art shows and county fairs. She was being recognized as a new talent in town. Instead of signing "Rosie" or "Rose" on her paintings, she signed them "Daisy McDonald."

Everyone started calling her Daisy, and it was difficult for me to change from Rosie to Daisy, so I just started calling her honey or sweetheart. To this day, she continues to paint and her paintings hang in art galleries and in private collections all over the United States. I'm very proud of her.

After I was retired a few years, I became a private investigator. I worked as a private eye for three years and it became a very boring job. The excitement and adrenalin rushes were not there. Divorces, child custody, and workman's compensation cases did not interest me.

In 1981, Rosie and I went via Washington, D.C. to visit my mother in Vinalhaven, Maine. Before I retired, I made it a point to visit my mother at least every five years. Now that she was growing older we tried to make it every two years.

In Washington, we toured the White House and also Arlington National Cemetery and President Kennedy's grave. As we watched the "Eternal Flame" of his torch flutter in the slight breeze, I bowed my head and said a silent prayer. Reading the inscriptions brought a flood of memories from that tragic day in Dallas so many years ago. In my mind, I still had unanswered questions with no satisfaction as to *why* this great man was struck down by an insignificant little punk!

As I stood there, my mind was running reel-to-reel like a motion picture projector seeing flashing images: the Zapruder film; the image of the movie actor Van Heflin when I glanced at the big screen of the Texas Theater; entering from the exit curtains; the struggle with Oswald, and the fight to take his pistol and subdue him; the crowd outside the theater; my friend and fellow police officer, Frank Williams, wiping the blood from my face; the scene of the Tippit murder and his drying blood on the asphalt street. And finally, the endless re-runs of Jack Ruby killing Oswald. I realized at that moment those images were branded in my memory forever.

Most summers Rose and I either drove or flew to Maine to be with my aging mother. She was totally blind and living alone. Her husband, Norman Calderwood, died in a VA Hospital in 1958. Also, that same year my father, Biddy McDonald died. In 1964, mother married again to Lawrence Cole, and they were married nearly fifteen years before he died in 1979. Mother was left alone once again. These were the reasons we tried to be with her each summer and to help as much as we could. She had to place her hand over the stove's burner to know if it was on or not.

My brother, Charles, moved to the island and married an island girl, Jean Kelwick. After nine years of marriage they were blessed with a baby boy. They continued to be blessed, having three children, two boys and a girl—John, Jimmy, and Patricia. They checked on mother a few times a week. In winter, they checked more often.

I had not been around mother very much because of the distances between us. Now that I was retired, I wanted to renew our relationship. Both of my grandparents had died in the 1960s. My grandmother, Laura, died of liver cancer in 1961. My grandfather suffered a crippling stroke and died in a nursing home in 1968. Except for my two daughters, my mother and brother were my only living relatives.

Then in 1988 my brother, Charles, died of lung cancer. Mother was really left alone, except for my sister-in-law, Jean.

My nephews and niece had left the island and were attending colleges, getting married and starting their own families.

My youngest daughter, Michelle, went through a divorce in Dallas and decided to be near us in Hot Springs. Several years later, my oldest daughter, Vicki, also went through a divorce in Dallas and moved to Hot Springs. Vicki left a high paying job, but found she could not find a comparable job in Hot Springs.

She decided to move to Vinalhaven, Maine to try to help my ailing, blind mother and to give her love, comfort, and companionship in her declining years. As she had never driven to Maine, I decided to go with her on this two thousand mile journey. We set out with her Ford Escort, loaded inside and out with her belongings. She wanted to drive all the way for the experience. We arrived at the ferry terminal after three days. Vinalhaven Island is located thirteen miles off the rocky coast of Rockland, Maine.

Vicki settled in an upstairs bedroom of her grandmother's house, and the two of them began to get reacquainted. When Vicki was born, mother travelled by train from Maine to Indiana to be with Sally for the birth. Mother had a special love for Vicki after she had helped Sally with the birth, and stayed two weeks with Vicki. I was in the Air Force at the time, stationed outside Rockville, Indiana.

Vicki was going to be with mother, and I was relieved. The following year, Vicki started dating an islander, David Moyer. They fell in love, and in May 1991 Rosie and I drove to Maine to attend their wedding. After the beautiful wedding, we spent several weeks with my mother, doing some needed work around the house and attending to her needs. We were both aware mother's health was rapidly failing.

Returning home, I told Rosie I had a premonition that mother might not make it through the harsh winter on the island trying to manage for herself. With all the goodness in her heart, Rosie said, "You better make plans to go and spend the winter with your mother."

On November 19, 1991, I flew to Maine to be with her. On December 4th at 4:00 p.m., I made an afternoon snack of coffee and a sandwich for her. Mother was eating and suddenly she put her hand up to the right side of her head, and cried out, "Oh, my head!" She slumped in her chair, where she always sat, and I jumped up, holding her in my arms as she took her last breath. Holding and gently rocking her, I tried to let her know I was there, and that she was not alone. She was with God now, and would never be alone again. She was eighty-seven-years-old.

I called Vicki and told her mother had just died and to send someone. She called the medical center where Jean, my sister-in-law, was the administrator. She and the doctor came immediately and the doctor pronounced her. Vicki and David arrived almost at the same time. The doctor said the body couldn't be moved until the undertaker came from the mainland the following day. Jean and the doctor had brought a body bag. We placed mother inside the body bag, and then placed it upon her bed in the bedroom. The doctor quietly closed the door.

I called Rosie and gave her the bad news and she said, "Honey, are you going to be alright?"

With a tremble in my voice, I said, "Yes, sweetheart, I'll be okay. I want you and Michelle to take the next plane and be with me and Vicki."

Rosie said they would be there as soon as they could leave.

Vicki and David wanted me to stay with them that night, but I said I'd rather stay near mother and not leave her alone. I opened the bedroom door, and sat at the table throughout the night without sleeping, silently keeping watch over my dear mother. When morning finally came, Vicki and David came to see me, and tried to get me to eat breakfast, but I had no appetite.

At 10:30 a.m. the ferryboat landed, bringing the undertakers with their gray hearse. They gently lifted mother and took her away. It was the middle of winter and the ground was frozen; they could not open a grave until the spring thaw. They had to keep the body in cold storage until then.

That night we had a heavy snowfall and by morning it was a blizzard. Vicki, David, and I met the one and only ferryboat from the mainland that morning to meet Rosie and Michelle. When they finally arrived, it was snowing so hard and thick, I couldn't distinguish the passengers getting off the ferry. All of them looked like bundled Eskimos. Vicki finally spotted Rosie and Michelle, and we all ran to them, gathering them up in our arms, kissing their cold, red lips and rosy cheeks.

The following day was Saturday, and the funeral home brought mother back to the island, where we had the funeral services in the Union Church. We said our sad goodbyes. Mother had lived on the island of Vinalhaven, Maine for forty-six years.

We returned to Vinalhaven the following spring for mother's memorial service and internment. In April 1992 she was buried next to her husband, Norman Calderwood, at Brown's Head Light Cemetery where she could always sleep to the intermittent soft ringing of the bell buoy protecting the thoroughfare between North Haven Island and Vinalhaven Island.

The following day, my sister-in-law, Jean, came to mother's house with mother's Will. After reading it, I was terribly disappointed. Several years before my brother, Charles, had died, he and I discussed that we would split her estate evenly. But mother had changed her Will in 1987, leaving me a grandchild's share amounting to one-sixth and the remainder went to my sister-in-law, Jean, and her three children, including mother's house. I couldn't believe my mother had reduced me to grandchild status, instead of her only living son. To my dying day, I will never understand her reasons why but so it goes.

26

THE CLINTONS

IN THE PAST, I have received a variety of recognition in the form of letters and awards from everyday people—judges, politicians, and dignitaries from all over the United States. And, I am very honored and proud to be recognized for arresting and capturing the accused assassin of President John F. Kennedy.

In July 1993, I finally wrote a letter to President Bill Clinton, asking why I had never been recognized by any president for my actions that tragic day in Dallas, Texas, in some small way. Not for me personally. But for a legacy for my children and my grandchildren. I have included a copy of this letter in my notes, intermixed with all the pictures in this book. I also included a copy of the letter that my wife, Rose, wrote to President Clinton in my notes.

In the fall of 1995, Roger Clinton came to Hot Springs for a book signing of his book, "Growing Up Clinton." We went to the signing for an autograph. I was standing at the end of a table watching Roger Clinton signing copies of his book with Jim Moore. Jim looked familiar and I suddenly realized he wasn't just the co-author of Roger's book, but he had also written *Conspiracy of One: The Definitive Book on the Kennedy Assassination.*

His book was one of the most factual books written on the assassination. I went over to Jim and introduced myself, and before I could finish, he recognized me by saying, "You're Nick McDonald. You arrested Oswald!" He took my hand and gave me a big hug, and said, "I heard that you had moved to Hot Springs. I'm so glad to have finally met you."

Smiling I said, "I'm really glad to have met you. I read your book and liked every word about the assassination."

Jim stood back, looked at my face and said, "Do you still have the scar from the fight with Oswald?"

I pointed to the side of my left eye and cheek and said, "Yeah. After nearly thirty-two years, I still have this reminder of our little fracas. Can you believe it?"

We exchanged business cards. Jim was busy collecting for Roger's book, and I turned to go back to the end of the autograph table. Dick Kelley, Roger's stepfather, was talking with my wife, Daisy. Shaking hands, we exchanged greetings and I returned to the table next to Roger Clinton. When Daisy finally got her turn, I handed Roger my signed business card and an 8 x 10 autographed photograph of me holding Oswald's pistol.

Roger put my business card in his shirt pocket and stood up from his chair, and grabbed my hand, saying with a broad smile, "It's a great honor to meet you! Thank you so much. It's really a thrill to meet you. I'll bet you and Jim have a lot to talk about!"

I answered, "It's a pleasure to meet you too, Roger. I already spoke with Jim while you were busy signing autographs."

Roger handed the brown envelope to Jim containing the autographed photo I gave him. Jim called out to me, "Say Nick, will you send me an autographed photo, too? My address is on the business card I gave you."

I said, "You bet Jim, I'll send you one just as soon as I can get more prints made."

BY THIS TIME, Daisy handed our book for Roger to sign. There is a wonderful, but sad story about Roger's mother, Virginia Clinton Kelley.

Daisy was commissioned to paint a horse racing scene for Virginia early in December 1993, by Ralph Wilson, owner of the Buffalo Bills football team. Mr. Wilson and Virginia had become close friends in the last few years. She had invited Ralph to attend horse racing at Oaklawn Park in Hot Springs and in turn he invited her to attend the Super Bowl when the Bills went in January 1993.

Ralph wanted the painting to be a Christmas present for Virginia because she loved horses and horse racing. The commission was requested much too late to be completed by Christmas, but Daisy sent a beautiful card to Virginia. Daisy explained in the card the painting was in the works and almost finished.

The very night Virginia Clinton Kelley died, Daisy put the last brush of paint to Virginia's canvas. In March 1994, Daisy presented the finished painting to Virginia's husband, Dick Kelley. To this day, it hangs in a special place in the home Virginia and Dick Kelley shared.

As Roger Clinton signed our book, he mentioned to Daisy that he had seen and admired the painting and was thrilled to meet the artist. Tears came in Roger's eyes as we were speaking of his mother, Virginia, remembering the sparkle in her personality.

I had a good friend, Mary Ann Masterson, who was a member of the Virginia Clinton Kelly Democratic Women's Club and they had planned a trip to Washington, D.C. to meet President Clinton.

I got an idea to send an autographed photograph to President Clinton like the one I gave to his brother Roger Clinton in 1995. I had been invited to give a speech at the Rotary Club in my hometown of Camden, Arkansas, about the arrest of Oswald. The local newspaper was there and the Ouachita County Historical Society wrote a lengthy article about me. They printed a booklet called *The Quarterly* and included my story. I autographed the booklet and included it with my photograph.

Mary Ann assured me she would hand it directly to President Clinton. In July 2000, I received a personal letter from President Bill Clinton, thanking me for the inscribed copy of *The Quarterly*.

I believe I finally received some recognition from a sitting President for my actions in Dallas, Texas on that tragic day, November 22, 1963 when President John F. Kennedy was assassinated by the accused assassin, Lee Harvey Oswald.

27
40TH ANNIVERSARY

GETTING READY TO attend church, I was in the shower, and suddenly I was remembering the shower I took on November 22, 1963, preparing to report for my 7:00 a.m. patrol duty.

Not a day goes by without remembering that fatalistic day in Dallas, but today had a significant meaning to me. I wasn't the wiry young man of thirty-five anymore, rather I was a seventy-five. Fresh in my memory was the continuing struggle to overcome my near death by a frenzied assassin. To me that day remains as vivid and real, as though it were today. I've had many sleepiness nights and endless days going over and over the events of that day. I always asked myself questions I had no satisfactory answer to in my mind. Could I have done anything that would have made a difference? My conclusive answer is always *no!*

One thing I am proud of—I chose not to shoot and kill Oswald. I realize now the gravity that moment could have caused me and my family. I probably would have been charged with murder or a wrongful death even though it would have been in self-defense. In the ensuing days, months and even years, I probably would have been condemned for not allowing Oswald to live, and eventually tell the whole truth about his actions.

But, Jack Ruby took it upon himself to silence the assassin forever. Anyhow, the things I did in arresting Lee Harvey Oswald, as one reporter commented, proved to be the only thing that was done right throughout the three day ordeal. In a flashing blast of gunfire, Jack Ruby had destroyed what I had accomplished. Oswald was brought in alive for questioning to allow the scales of justice to balance the wrongs. I had fulfilled my duty as a police officer, which is expected and demanded by the law and order of justice.

Now after forty years of investigating, testing, analyzing and interviewing witnesses and non-witnesses, nothing has revealed any credible conspiracy evidence. Oliver Stone, the movie director, based the movie *JFK* on the conspiracy book written by Jim Garrison, District Attorney of New Orleans. Together they have convinced ninety percent of the American people that they are now the official historians of the Kennedy assassination.

They are telling lies to make you believe it is the truth. Oliver Stone reminds me of P.T. Barnum who made the statement, "A sucker is born every minute!" It is awfully hard for me to believe that ninety percent of the American people are "suckers!" I think it's a real tragedy that school children may accept the movie *JFK* as fact, instead of being taught the truth.

What has happening at the Ford Theater in Washington, D.C. now happens in Dallas at the assassination site. Recently, my nephew visited the site and said two guys were in front of the Texas School Book Depository selling souvenirs and tabloid pictorials. One was standing on the sidewalk, and the other guy was on the infamous grassy knoll, pointing out where the gunman was standing. They were telling their versions of the assassination, and what happened that day to the wandering tourists—confusing them even more.

What a terrible shame to turn a place of history into a circus with clowns and magicians without a tent.

On the fortieth anniversary of John F. Kennedy's assassination there was little fanfare and commemoration in Dallas according to news footage. Only a handful of locals and curious tourists milled around Dealey Plaza. Fewer and fewer care about President Kennedy's assassination because half of the population in the United States wasn't even born at that time in history.

All they have been subjected to are the tainted image of a president portrayed by tabloids, as involved in illicit sexual affairs, and colored with the stigma of the Bay of Pigs. How quickly everyone forgot how he successfully diverted a nuclear holocaust with communist Russia. He accomplished this by being a strong-willed, intelligent leader who led this nation for only one thousand days.

For years Dallas' residents were ashamed and angry that Kennedy had been killed in Dallas. Like Dallas, did the other cities suffer after they experienced assassinations like Washington, D.C.; Buffalo, New York; Miami, Florida; Memphis, Tennessee; and Los Angles, California? I think not.

Over the last forty years, the city of Dallas has buried its shame and has regained pride with a professional football franchise the Dallas Cowboys (America's Team) and the trials and tribulations of South Fork Ranch in the television series, *Dallas.*

Even if the commemorations have dissipated over the years, those who were there or had some part in the tragic events will never forget those terrible days of November 1963.

I was in Dallas at Dealey Plaza and the Sixth Floor Museum on the fortieth anniversary of the assassination, walking down

Elm Street. Once again the flash memories filled my mind as I stood in front of the Texas School Book Depository building. That terrible day where I once stood with my rookie partner, and hearing the report J.D. Tippit had been gunned down. The memory caused tears to flood my eyes and a choking dryness in my throat.

Later that day, November 22, 2003, I finally granted a videotaped interview to the Sixth Floor Museum for their archives. The interview was taped for over an hour as I related my actions on that day, November 22, 1963, forty years ago to the day.

On that same day, I went to the Texas Theater to re-enact the arrest and capture of Lee Harvey Oswald to be developed for a documentary about my life. Memories of those awful four tragic days of November still cause a terrible hurt to wrap around my heart.

Lee Harvey Oswald holding one of his guns

Outside the theater where Oswald was captured

Left: Outside the theater where Oswald was captured, Top right: The lobby of the theater, Bottom right: The seat where Oswald was sitting when he was captured

Police officers and members of the media attempt to reconstruct what happened

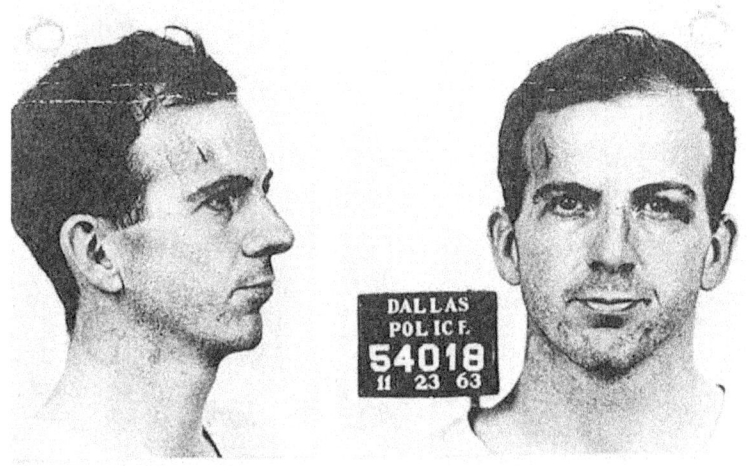

Lee Harvey Oswald's mugshot

The scar that was a result of the scuffle with the accused

The Homicide Bureau Office under guard while Oswald was interrogated

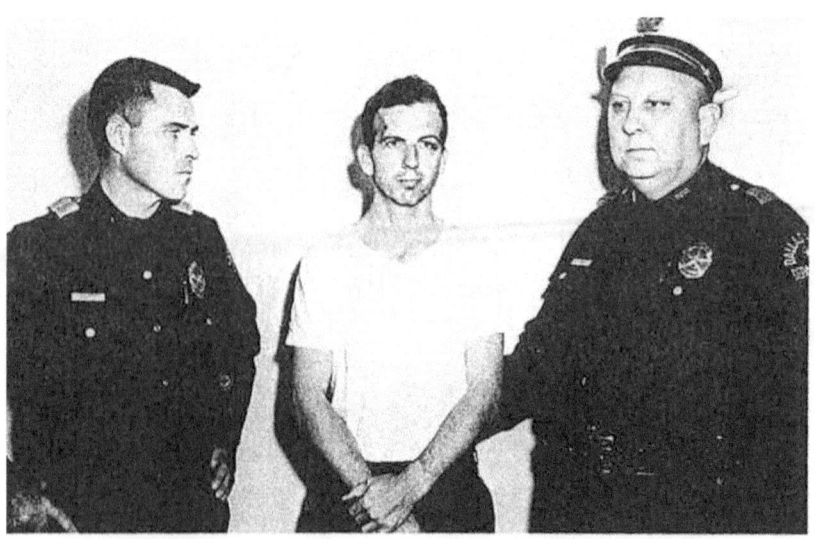

Oswald stands with Sergeant W.F. Warren, Jail Supervisor, and Officer T.V. Todd just before being processed in the Identification Bureau

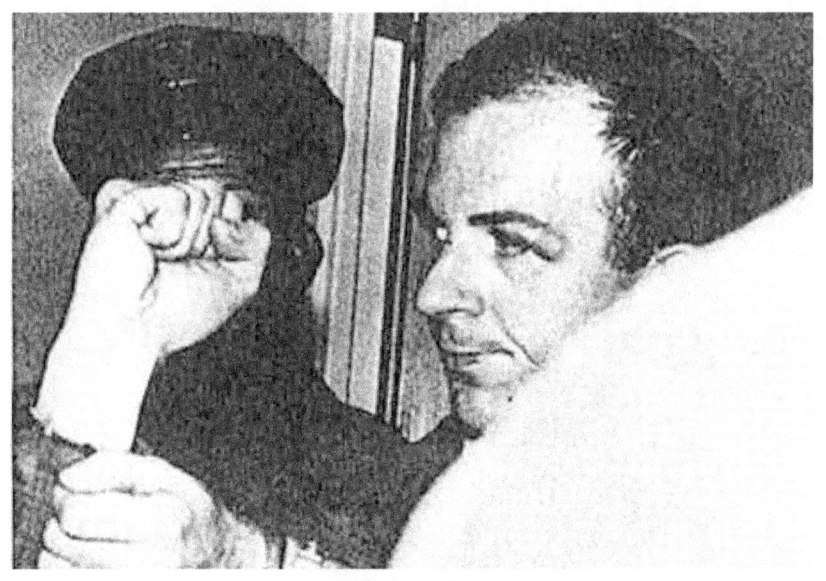

Even after arrest, Oswald remains defiant

Oswald taken to rest during an interrogation break

After being interrogated, Oswald is taken upstairs to the jail

Captain Will Fritz, head of the Dallas Homicide Bureau was in charge of Oswald's interrogation

Marina Oswald comes to the Dallas Jail to visit her husband

District Attorney Henry Wade interviewed by the press

Oswald interviewed by the press

POLICE DEPARTMENT
CITY OF DALLAS

ARREST REPORT
ON
INVESTIGATIVE PRISONER

1-1
5-9-¼

FIRST NAME	MIDDLE NAME	LAST NAME	DATE	TIME
LEE	HARVEY	OSWALD	11-22-63	1:40 PM

RACE: WHITE ☒ COLORED ☐ SEX: MALE ☒ FEMALE ☐ AGE: 24 DATE OF BIRTH: OCT. 18-39 HOME ADDRESS: 1026 N. BECKLEY

ADDRESS WHERE ARREST MADE: 231 W. JEFFERSON TYPE PREMISES: THEATRE

CHARGE: INV. MURDER & ASS'LT TO MURDER

HOW ARREST MADE: ON VIEW ☒ CALL ☐ WARRANT ☐

LOCATION OF OFFENSE: ASSAULT TO MURDER OFF # F85954

OTHER DETAILS OF THE ARREST:
This man shot and killed President John F. Kennedy and Police Officer J. D. Tippit. He also shot and wounded Governor John Connally.

Assault to Murder OFF # F85954

ARRESTING OFFICER: M.N. McDONALD I.D. NO: 1178
ARRESTING OFFICER: K.E. LYONS I.D. NO: 1226
OTHER OFFICER: LT. E.L. CUNNINGHAM
OTHER OFFICER: P.L. BENTLEY I.D. NO: 526

DATE: 11-22-63 DATE-TIME TO CO. JAIL: 11-24-11? PM

Officer M.N. McDonald 1178

The completed arrest report on Lee Harvey Oswald

THE ARREST AND CAPTURE OF LEE HARVEY OSWALD
BY OFFICER M.N."NICK" MCDONALD, 11/22/63

    As I approached the front of the Texas Theatre, police cars were already there and the officers had already entered through the front entrance.
    I wheeled around to the alley at the rear of the theatre. Officers were standing in the alley with shotguns raised, guarding the exit doors. Getting out of my police car, I decided to try opening the exit door. I started pulling, shaking and banging on the heavy metal door. Since it was an exit door, I realized it could be opened only from the inside. Suddenly, the door opened outward and two men in civilian suits quietly motioned for me to come in. One of the men was Johnny Brewer, whom I later learned was the witness who had observed a suspicious acting man dart into the theatre. The other man identified himself as an usher for the theatre.
    Entering, I went to the exit curtains to the left of the movie screen, with Johnny Brewer close behind. As I peeked through the heavy curtains out into the audience, Johnny, at my shoulder, pointed out the suspect. He was at the rear on the main floor, three rows from the partition of the lobby, quietly sitting in the second chair from the right center aisle.
    He was staring straight ahead, watching the movie, unconcerned, -- unconcerned of the sudden appearance of police officers that had entered the theatre, searching for a suspect in the murder of Officer J.D. Tippit.
    I noticed there were only 10 or 15 patrons for this, a Friday matinee showing of double bill features, "<u>Cry of Battle</u>" and "<u>War is Hell</u>"! How factual these titles would relate to reality, in just a few moments!
    I made my decision to try an act of diversion. I searched two men seated in the middle, near the front of the movie screen and nearest to me. Then, searched each person in turn as I got to them, before getting to him. I hoped this indirect approach would cause him to believe that I was not considering him and he would relax his guard.
    After a hasty search of the first two men, I started walking unhurriedly up the aisle toward him. Slowly, deliberately, I was closing the distance between us. Maybe, just maybe, I could prevent a stand-off and a shoot-out, if I could only get close enough! My pistol remained strapped in my holster. My hand was open and swinging freely along my side. My searching eyes were more concentrated on two others seated to my left, just a few steps from him. But, I had him in my peripheral vision. Detecting no movement or change in his position, nor was he even looking at me, I continued walking calmly up the aisle, trying to act as if I were going to pass him by. I had this strange sensation that everyone in the theatre had their eyes fixed on me and were watching my every move. I was almost there.
    Still no movement from him. The diversion was working. I was there now! I turned quickly into his row! Moving closer, I saw his empty hands were folded in his lap.

As he calmly looked up at me, I spoke with a strong voice of authority, "Get on your feet"! He realized he had waited too long to make a free and open move of aggression.
He stood slowly, as if in slow motion, facing the movie screen, blinking and turning his head to me. We were face to face. I stared into his icy cold, steel blue eyes. In an attempt to conceal his guilt, his expression changed to surprise and innocence, like that of a child caught with his hand in a cookie jar.
Without a command, he started bringing up both hands and in a voice of resignation, he spoke softly, "Well, it's all over now"! I thought he was giving up, and for a moment I was surprised at the simplicity of the arrest! I had him!
My hands started reaching for his waist to make the routine search of his person for a concealed weapon. His right hand had reached his shoulder level and his left hand had reached eye level. Suddenly, his left hand made a tight fist and it exploded between my eyes. I thought, "My God, this is it! He is not giving up after all"! The impact from his fist knocked my head back, momentarily catching me off balance and sent my police cap flying across the seats. With the same darting movement, his right hand went to his waist. With my left hand, I felt him pulling a pistol from underneath his shirt. An automatic reaction of aggression began with me physically, before my brain commanded me. He brought the pistol up to my chest, I grabbed for it with my left hand and grasped his pistol over the cylinder and hammer, with all the strength I could muster. I could feel the hammer glide under my hand, as he pulled the trigger. The returning hammer made a dull, audible snapping sound, as the firing pin struck the flesh of my left hand, between the thumb and forefinger. Bracing myself, I stood rigid, waiting for the bullet to penetrate my chest. Somehow, the miracle of my strength retarded the action of the cylinder and hammer. The bullet beneath the firing pin did not receive the full striking force and slightly dented the primer of the shell. I pivoted his pistol to the side and away from my body, and realized I was not shot. With a clutched fist, I hit him over his left eye, knocking him into the seat. With a lunge of desperation, I fell on top of him to cover him with my body.
Falling on him, I tried to smother his movements. I was in a desperate struggle to gain possession of his pistol. I knew that he could not hurt me with his fist, but I also knew that I could be seriously wounded or even killed by his pistol. Our arms and elbows were entangled with our twisting and turning bodies. My life depended on gaining complete control of his weapon. I somehow managed to grasp the handle of his pistol with my right hand and jerked it away from him. I shoved the muzzle into his stomach, and for a fleeting moment, I thought, "He tried to kill me and I'd be justified in killing him"!
But on second thought, "There is no need to shoot him, now that I have control of his weapon". I pulled the pistol away and handed it to a detective standing in the aisle. I called out to my fellow officers, "I've got him"!!!!!!

POLICE DEPARTMENT
CITY OF DALLAS
PD-JS-254

ARREST REPORT
ON
INVESTIGATIVE PRISONER

1ST NAME: LEE   MIDDLE NAME: HARVEY   LAST NAME: OSWALD   DATE: 11-22-63   TIME: 1:40 pm
RACE: WHITE ☒ COLORED ☐   SEX: MALE ☒ FEMALE ☐   AGE: 24   DATE OF BIRTH: OCT. 18-39   HOME ADDRESS: 1026 N. BECKLEY
ADDRESS WHERE ARREST MADE: 231 W. JEFFERSON   TYPE PREMISES: THEATRE
CHARGE: INV. MURDER + ASSLT TO MURDER
HOW ARREST MADE: VIEW ☒ CALL ☐ WARRANT ☐

OTHER DETAILS OF THE ARREST:
This man shot and killed President John F. Kennedy and Police Officer J. D. Tippit. He also shot and wounded Governor John Connally.

Assault to Murder Off # F85954

CHECK ALL ITEMS WHICH APPLY:
DRUNK ☐ DRINKING ☐ CURSED ☐ RESISTED ☐ FOUGHT ☐

ARRESTING OFFICER: M.N. McDONALD   I.D. NO. 1178   K.E. LYONS   I.D. NO. 1276
OTHER OFFICER: LT. Ed. CUNNINGHAM   P.I. BENTLEY   I.D. NO. 526
INVESTIGATION ASSIGNED TO: Fritz   CHARGE FILED: 2 cases murder   DATE: 11-22-63   DATE-TIME TO CO. JAIL: 11-24-11:20 am
RELEASED BY: DATE-TIME: Fritz   DATE-TIME: 11-22-63   COURT: 11-24-63   DATE: TIME: Fritz

NAME LEE HARVEY OSWALD
ALA ALEK JAMES HIDELL

SEX MALE RACE WHITE DPD # 54018 FBI # DPS #

AGE 24 HT 5-9 WT 140 HAIR BRN EYES BLUE COMP FAIR OCC STOCK WORK, ORDER FILLE

DATE AND PLACE OF BIRTH OCTOBER 18, 1939 NEW ORLEANS, LOUISIANA

PRESENT ADDRESS 1026 NORTH BECKLEY, DALLAS - 2515 WEST 5TH ST., IRVING, TEXAS

SCARS AND MARKS NONE

DATE OF ARREST NOVEMBER 22, 1963 CHARGE INV. MURDER & ASSAULT TO MURDER

ARRESTED BY M. N. McDONALD 1178 ARREST # 63-98155

PRINTED BY [signature] CLASSED BY SEARCHED BY

NEAREST RELATIVE AND ADDRESS WIFE-MARINA; TWO INFANT CHILDREN, 2515 W. 5TH, IRVING.

SIGNATURE

POLICE DEPARTMENT, DALLAS, TEXAS BUREAU OF IDENTIFICATION FORM 12

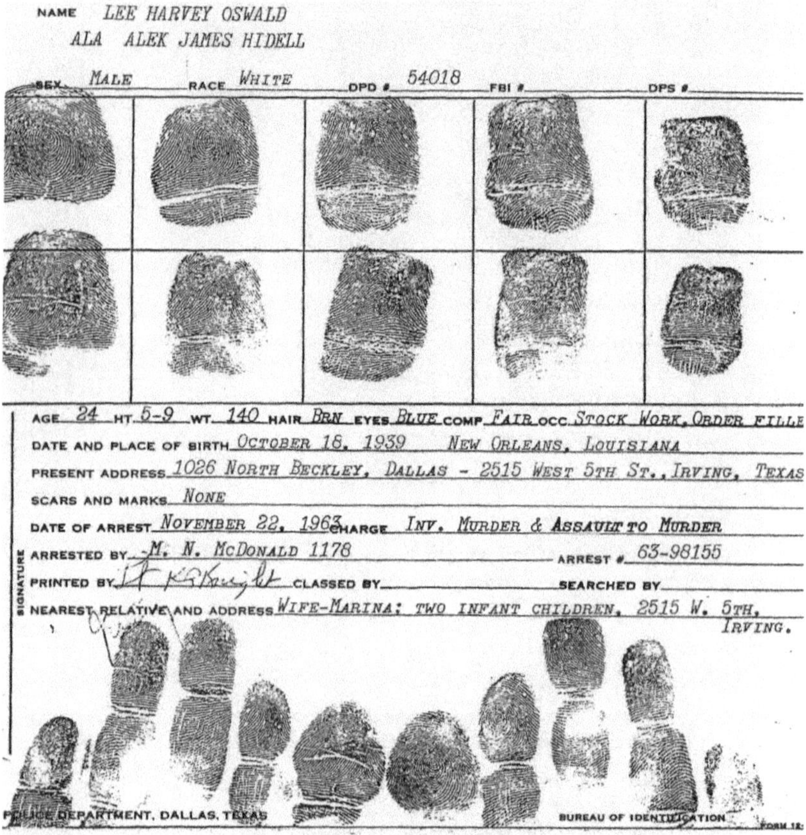

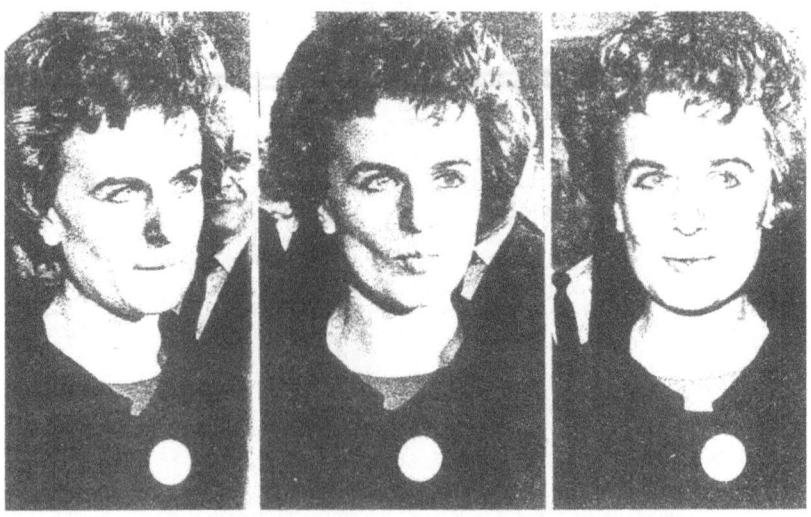

Marina Oswald told very unfavorable testimony to the Commission

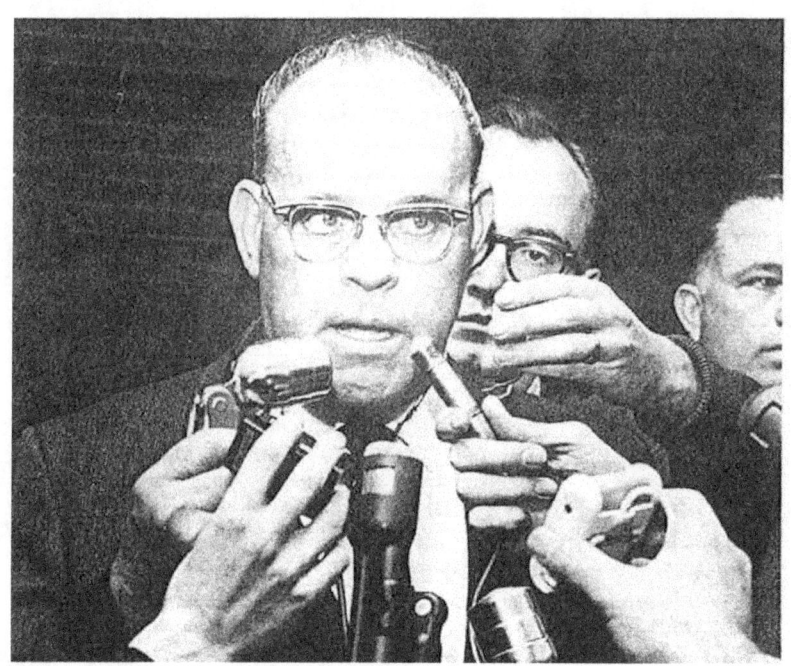
In a press interview Chief Curry explains the evidence linking Oswald to the assassination of John F. Kennedy

Jack Ruby makes his move to shoot Oswald

Lee Harvey Oswald crumples from the impact of Jack Ruby's shot

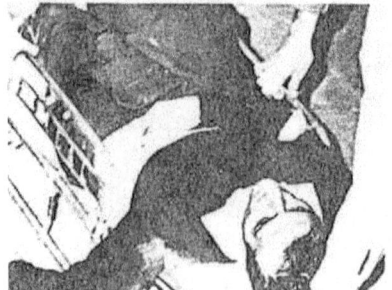

Oswald loaded into an ambulance minutes after the shooting

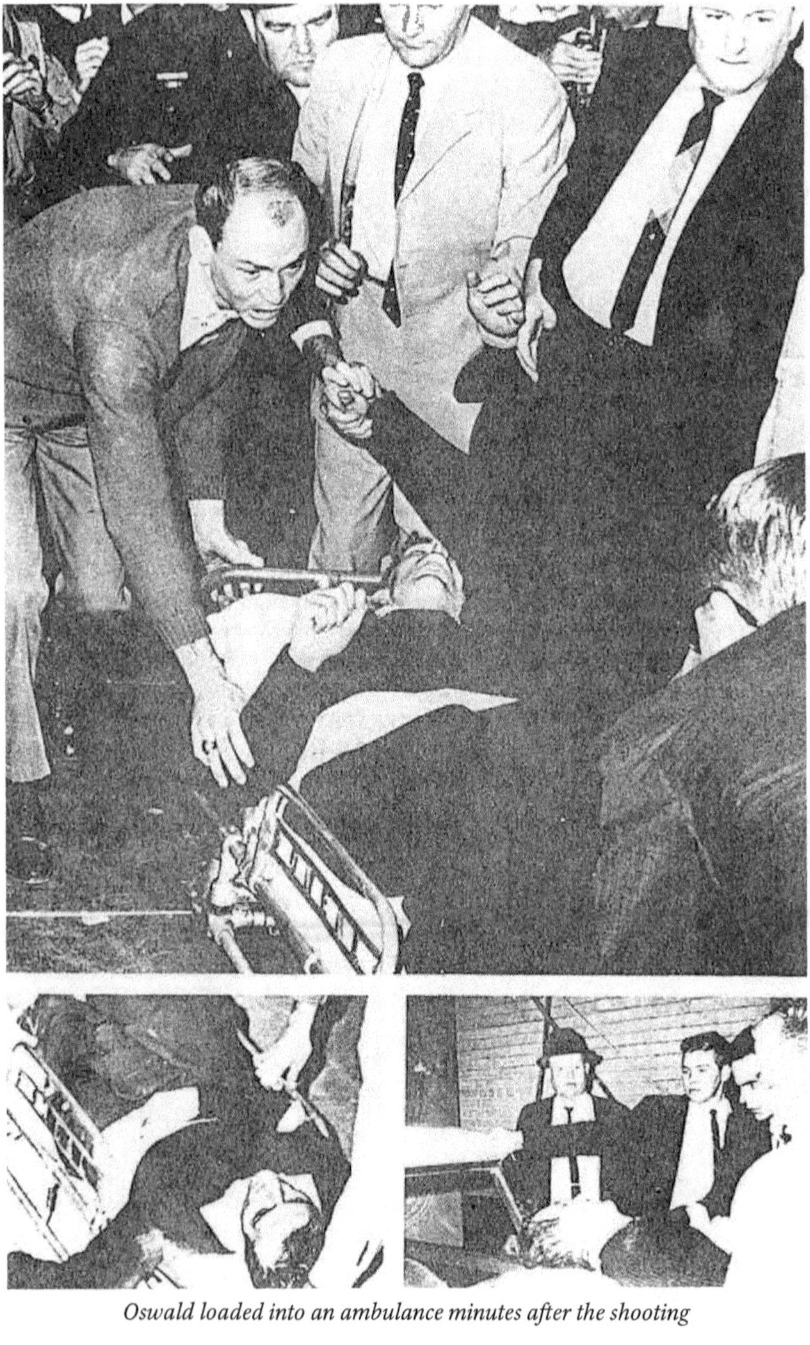

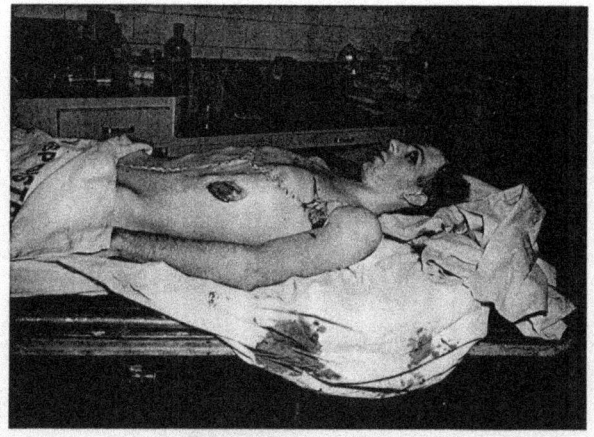

Autographed picture of the Oswald autopsy

The business card Jack Ruby passed out to various police officers prior to shooting Oswald

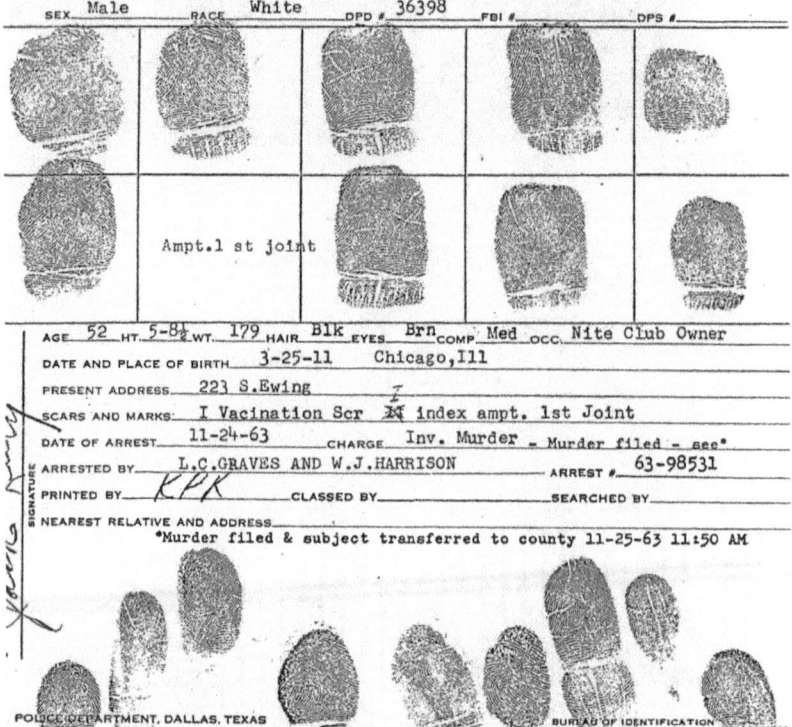

November 22, 1963

Captain W.P. Gannaway
Special Service Bureau

SUBJECT: Lee Harvey Oswald
605 Elsbeth Street

Sir:

On November 22, 1963, at approximately 2:50PM, the undersigned officer met Special Agent James Hosty of the Federal Bureau of Investigation in the basement of the City Hall.

At that time Special Agent Hosty related to this officer that the Subject was a member of the Communist Party, and that he was residing in Dallas.

The Subject was arrested for the murder of Officer J.D. Tippit and is a prime suspect in the assassination of President Kennedy.

The information regarding the Subject's affiliation with the Communist Party is the first information this officer has received from the Federal Bureau of Investigation regarding same.

Agent Hosty further stated that the Federal Bureau of Investigation was aware of the Subject and that they had information that this Subject was capable of committing the assassination of President Kennedy.

Respectfully submitted,

Jack Revill, Lieutenant
Criminal Intelligence Section

Sworn to and subscribed before me, this the 7th day of April, 1964.

FRANCES DOCK
Notary, Dallas County, Dallas, Texas

The sworn statement indicating that the F.B.I. knew of Oswald's presence in Dallas

PLEASE FILL OUT APPLICATION BLANK COMPLETELY............

NAME **Oswald Lee H** STREET & NUMBER **2515 W 5th S** TOWN **Irving**
LAST NAME FIRST

PHONE NO **BL3-1628** SOCIAL SECURITY NO **433-54-3937** AGE **23** WEIGHT **150** HEIGHT **5'9"**
PLACE OF BIRTH **New Orleans La.** HOW LONG LIVED IN DALLAS **Continuously**
FINISHED WHAT GRADE IN SCHOOL **11th** NAME SCHOOL **Arlington Heights** TOWN **Ft. Worth, Texas**
DID YOU ATTEND COLLEGE **No** HOW LONG **—** NAME COLLEGE
RACE **C** MARRIED (✓) OR SINGLE ( ) HOW MANY DEPENDENTS **2 dependents**
WHERE DID YOU LAST WORK **USMC (three years)** NATURE OF WORK **Air Wing**
REASON FOR LEAVING LAST JOB **Honorable Discharge**
HOW LONG DID YOU WORK ON YOUR LAST JOB **Three Years**
WHERE IS YOUR FATHER EMPLOYED **Dead** NATURE OF WORK **—**
IS YOUR MOTHER EMPLOYED **Yes** NATURE OF WORK **Practical Nurse**
MEMBER OF ORGANIZATIONS: CHURCH LODGE VETERAN

HAVE YOU ANY PHYSICAL DEFECTS (ANSWER YES OR NO) IF ANSWER IS YES STATE WHAT THEY ARE:
No

DO YOU ROOM AND BOARD **No** DO YOU LIVE WITH PARENTS **No**

SHOULD YOU LIKE TO MENTION SOME OF YOUR SPECIAL ABILITIES YOU WOULD LIKE COMPANY TO KNOW IN CONSIDERING YOUR APPLICATION USE THE THREE LINES BELOW.

Clerical (Accounting) Work in Military Service
Experienced with Ditto, Adding, and Some Typing
Machine and Filing System

DATE OF APPLICATION
Oct 15, 1963

SIGNATURE OF APPLICANT **Lee H. Oswald** BONDED
By Brear DATE 2-11-64
INITIALS S

2965-15

Oswald's employment application for the Texas School Book Depository

TREASURY DEPARTMENT
UNITED STATES SECRET SERVICE
FIELD FORCE

Dallas
P.O. LOCK BOX NO. 2089

Dallas, Texas, 75221
December 26, 1963

Mr. Jesse Curry,
Chief of Police,
Dallas, Texas.

Re: Attempted assassination of
General Edwin A. Walker, Dallas, Texas.

Dear Chief Curry:

    The following information was developed by this Service relative to the attempted assassination of Retired General Edwin A. Walker, in Dallas, Texas, on April 10, 1963.

    On December 2, 1963, there was received from the Irving Police Department, Irving, Texas, some belongings of Mrs. Marina Oswald which had been brought to the Police Station by Mrs. Ruth Paine with whom Mrs. Marina Oswald had been living. When these articles were examined in the Secret Service Office there was found in a book a note written in very poor Russian which was in the handwriting of Lee Harvey Oswald and which apparently was instructions to his wife what she should do in the event that he should be alive and taken as a prisoner.

    On December 3, 1963 Mrs. Marina Oswald was questioned about this note by one of our special agents who speaks Russian and she stated that this note had nothing to do with the assassination of President Kennedy and that the note was written by her husband prior to his attempted assassination of former General Walker, whom she classified as the head of the Fascist Organization in the United States and who lived in Dallas, Texas, when they, the Oswalds, lived on Neely Street in Dallas; that the note, together with a Post Office key was left on a dresser of their bedroom and after reading the note she was afraid that her husband was planning on doing something dreadful due to his hate for the Fascist Organizations and their beliefs. She also stated that when her husband returned home late that night he was very nervous and finally told her that he shot Walker with his rifle and that it was best for everybody that he got rid of him.

    Mrs. Oswald further stated that when it was learned the next day from radios and newspapers that the rifle shot fired by an unknown person had missed Walker that she decided to keep the note as a threat against her husband so that he would not mistreat her again (it was determined that when the Oswalds lived on Neely Street that people living downstairs beneath the Oswalds had complained to the landlord about Oswald beating his wife) which he had promised not to do. She further commented that she did not report this matter to the Police as she loved her husband and particularly that she did not report it to the Police on account of their child. She stated, however, that had the shot hit General Walker, that she would have reported the matter to the Police. She was apprehensive about this matter being reported to the Police because she had a fear of being taken in custody by the Police because the information contained in this letter regarding the General Walker incident and the rifle would show that she had not told the Police all she knew when she was shown and questioned about the rifle that was used to assassinate President Kennedy.

On Dec. 10, 1963, our Special Agent had an opportunity to question Mrs. Marina Oswald more in detail regarding the General Walker incident and she stated that Lee Harvey Oswald told her that once before taking the shot at General Walker on April 10, 1963, he had gone to the Walker residence for the same purpose but he had changed his mind as the place had not looked just right for him and that 3 days prior to April 10, 1963, he took his rifle out of the house and buried it in a field near Walker's house. Mrs. Oswald further stated that upon her husband's return to the house after he had tried to kill General Walker and telling her about it that 3 days later she saw him taking his military green raincoat for the purpose of wrapping the rifle and bringing it home. However, she stated that when he returned home she did not see the rifle but several days later she saw the rifle on a shelf in the apartment where he always kept it. She also stated that the evening her husband shot at Walker he told her that the church which is located near the Walker house had some gathering; that there was plenty of noise and that after the shooting of Walker he buried the rifle in the same place.

Mrs. Marina Oswald further stated that Lee Harvey Oswald told her after reading in newspapers that some young man saw an automobile containing three men pulling away from the scene of the shooting, that the Americans always think they should have a car to get away from the scene of the crime but that he had rather use his feet to do so rather than a car, and he stated that he had taken a bus to go to the Walker residence and that he took a different bus to return home after the shooting.

Mrs. Marina Oswald was questioned as to how she was able to explain to her mother-in-law, Mrs. Marguerite Oswald, concerning the attempted assassination of General Walker by her husband, and she replied that she did to the best of her knowledge of the English language, and that no one else knew about the shooting at General Walker by her husband excepting her and her mother-in-law.

Very truly yours,

Forrest V. Sorrels,
Special Agent in Charge.

FVS:VS

PRESIDENT'S COMMISSION ON THE ASSASSINATION OF PRESIDENT KENNEDY

CHIEF JUSTICE EARL WARREN, *Chairman*

SENATOR RICHARD B. RUSSELL
SENATOR JOHN SHERMAN COOPER
REPRESENTATIVE HALE BOGGS

REPRESENTATIVE GERALD R. FORD
MR. ALLEN W. DULLES
MR. JOHN J. MCCLOY

J. LEE RANKIN, *General Counsel*

Assistant Counsel

FRANCIS W. H. ADAMS
JOSEPH A. BALL
DAVID W. BELIN
WILLIAM T. COLEMAN, Jr.
MELVIN ARON EISENBERG
BURT W. GRIFFIN
LEON D. HUBERT, Jr.

ALBERT E. JENNER, Jr.
WESLEY J. LIEBELER
NORMAN REDLICH
W. DAVID SLAWSON
ARLEN SPECTER
SAMUEL A. STERN
HOWARD P. WILLENS*

Staff Members

PHILLIP BARSON
EDWARD A. CONROY
JOHN HART ELY
ALFRED GOLDBERG
MURRAY J. LAULICHT
ARTHUR MARMOR
RICHARD M. MOSK
JOHN J. O'BRIEN
STUART POLLAK
ALFREDDA SCOBEY
CHARLES N. SHAFFER, Jr.
LLOYD L. WEINREB

Featured in "Parade," March 1964

Thomas "Boston" Corbett, the man who shot James Wilkes Booth

The Dallas Morning News

DALLAS, TEXAS, FRIDAY, APRIL 24, 1964

—Dallas News Staff Photo.

Officer McDonald, Mrs. J. D. Tippit with Chief Curry.

Three Posthumous Awards Made to Patrolman Tippit

POLICE CROSS--MEDAL OF HONOR--AWARD OF HONOR
OFFICER McDONALD--MEDAL OF HONOR--AWARD OF HONOR

Award of Honor article from "The Dallas Morning News," April 1964

Holding a revolver owned by Lee Harvey Oswald

1964
POLICE HALL OF FAME HONORS

FOR VALOR

Patrolman Maurice "Nick" McDonald, Dallas Police Department, Texas. On the fateful day of November 22nd, 1963, Patrolman McDonald was on patrol when the police radio called all cars to the scene of President John F. Kennedy's assassination. A short time later, at a patrol point, he heard a civilian report over the police radio that an officer from car ten had been shot. He knew that it was Patrolman J. D. Tippit (awarded the posthumous Medal of Merit for Valor). Officer McDonald responded to this new call and was directed to a movie theatre where the suspected killer was hiding. Officer McDonald and other uniformed Dallas policemen entered the movie house and the lights were turned up. A witness pointed out Lee Oswald who was sitting in the last row. Making his way there McDonald told Oswald to stand up and began to search him. Oswald reached for a hidden snub nose S&W revolver and a terrific struggle ensued in a fight for the revolver.

Oswald hit Officer McDonald several times, both with his fist and the revolver. Finally Oswald put the gun into Officer McDonald's chest and pulled the trigger. McDonald, seeing this about to happen, prevented the hammer from striking hard and although the hammer fell the weight was too light to set off the round. By then McDonald, in a last moment struggle, pulled the pistol away and other officers pulled Oswald off him.

Officer McDonald's extreme bravery in facing a man known to have already killed a fellow officer and suspected of killing the President, without firing a shot and facing certain death in a struggle with the suspect is the basis for this Award of Valor.

On May 2d, 1964, at Chicago, Illinois, the Medal of Valor, a check for $250.00, and a citation will be presented to Officer Mc-

PATROLMAN M. N. McDONALD

Donald who played so important a part in history on November 22nd, 1963. His name and photo will be preserved in the Police Hall of Fame in honor of his bravery and heroism.

HARRIS B. TUTTLE

FOR DISTINGUISHED SERVICE

Harris B. Tuttle, Law Enforcement Consultant for Photography of the Eastman Kodak Company, Rochester, New York for distinguished service in the field of scientific investigations.

Harris B. Tuttle is perhaps the most outstanding expert in the world in the use and adaption of photography in criminal investigation. His over forty years of experience has been made available without charge to law enforcement officers nation-wide.

Author of many articles and books on the uses of photography, both still and motion pictures, in police work, he is also active in many police organizations; the International Association for Identification, the International Association of Police Chiefs, National Sheriffs' Association, International Association of Arson Investigators, American Society of Criminalities, and Associate Editor of Valor Magazine.

He has pioneered the use of color photography in police work which has made a marked advance in identification and use in the court room.

His citation reads in part: "for his unselfish devotion to the science of law enforcement photography which has greatly aided the law enforcement profession in their efforts to prevent crime and to apprehend criminals in acts against society. His experiments and techniques, which he has shared freely with law enforcement officers, have made his contribution to his nation in the war against crime a tribute to his image as a great American."

The National Police Hall of Fame each year selects one man who has contributed to the law enforcement field and we are certain that identification officers and superiors in the field will join with us in this tribute to our candidate for the Distinguished Service Award for 1964.

Receiving the Medal of Valor at the Playboy Club

Receiving Playboy award from Benny Dunn at the Police Hall of Fame dinner in Chicago

Another memory featured in "The Playboy Club Magazine"

Approaching the speakers' table at the 1964 Hall of Fame Awards Dinner in Chicago, Illinois

Being greeted in Denver prior to being the guest of honor at the Police Protective Association of Colorado

Receiving the Medal of Honor and Dallas Citizens Traffic Commission Award of Honor alongside Sally

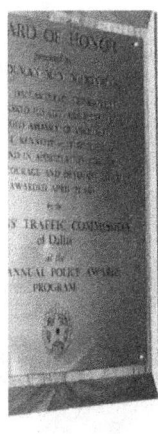

Enjoying a cup of coffee and the morning paper

Leaving the Warren Commission Hearings with Senator John Cooper of Kentucky, Eugene Boone, and Marrion Baker

At home with Sally

Posing with wife Sally and daughters, Michelle and Vicki

Rose Daisy McDonald
405 Fleet Street
Hot Springs, AR. 71913-6048
(501) 623-6777

May 10, 1994

The President of the United States
The White House
1600 Pennslyvania Avenue
Washington, D.C. 20006

Dear Mr. President:

I am enclosing a photograph of me presenting a painting to Mr. Dick Kelley. Mr. Ralph Wilson, owner of the NFL, Buffalo Bills, commissioned me to paint this horse racing scene for your mother, Mrs. Virginia Kelley. I was happy to do this with loving kindness.

The night your mother died, I had put the last brush stroke to her painting. The next day when I had heard that she had passed away the night before, I was overcome with grief. Not only had this dear lady left us, but you lost a friend and a mother. I was very sad that she never had the opportunity to see the finished work. I know she would have loved it.

Mr. President, I would also like to tell you about my husband, Maurice "Nick" McDonald. Nick was the Dallas Police Officer that arrested Lee Harvey Oswald, the assassin of President John F. Kennedy. I would appreciate it very much if you would write to him and let him know how you feel about his accomplishments.

Also, would you please honor us with an autographed photograph. I know he would be honored to hear from you, because he is a loyal supporter of yours and thinks highly of your efforts to make our country a better, safer place to live. We are with you and Mrs. Clinton 100%.

Respectfully,

Rose Daisy McDonald

(COPY)

Daisy and Virginia's painting in her home

Daisy presenting Dick Kelley with Virginia's painting

Working the desk in April 1978

Fulfilling the duties of the Supervisor Sergeant of the Dallas Police

The last days on the job before retirement, July 1980

Posing with Assemblyman Patrick Diegan, Mayor Dan Gallagher, Deputy Police Chief Tulio Capparelli, and Police Chief Robert Merkler

With former NYPD detective and movie/television producer Sonny Grosso

Receiving a proclamation from Police Chief Robert Merkler

Signing some memorabilia

Speaking to the crowd

During the 40th anniversary of the Kennedy assassination

Maurice "Nick" McDonald
405 Fleet Street
Hot Springs, AR. 71913
(501) 623-6777

July 21, 1993

The President of the United States
The White House
Washington, D.C. 20006

Dear Mr. President:

Even though I have not met you, I feel I know you well. I sincerely hope that someday my wife and I can meet you and Mrs. Clinton. For now, I want to tell you how much we have admired you as a family man and a respected, devoted Governor of our State, all those years you gave of yourself to make Arkansas a better place to live. According to my wife, Rose Daisy, and I, you have a great future for our country and an opportunity to fulfill President Kennedy's ambitions for our nation.

I was born and bred a native Arkansan (Ouachita County, Camden, Arkansas) and was raised in the same town of Senator David Pryor and knew him as a boy. After I served four years in the U.S. Air Force, during the Korean Conflict, I went to Dallas, Texas and became a member of the Dallas Police Department (1955). I served as a Police Officer for twenty-five years and retired back to my home state in August, 1980. While I was serving as a Police Officer on November 22, 1963, I arrested Lee Harvey Oswald, the accused assassin of President John F. Kennedy.

The reason I am writing to you is to apprise you of how our government has, some how, passed me by without recognizing what I was able to accomplish on that dreadful day in Dallas. I arrested the man, the Warren Commission concluded, was responsible for the death of a President of the United States. I have been ignored by our government! I realize I was just doing my duty, but everything that I did that day was done because it was my decision. I was not told or ordered by anyone to go into that theater. This was my own devotion to duty, and I felt this was my responsibility as a public servant and police officer to track down the man responsible for killing Officer J.D. Tippit. I did not realize that Oswald was considered suspect in the assassination until he was taken to the offices of the Homicide Division of the police department. When I became aware of this, I was elated that I had captured the prime suspect in the assassination in just Ninety-Minutes after it had occurred! I was feeling good that I came out of it alive for my own family, since he had tried to kill me!

Would it be presumptious of me to ask, if there could be a token of acknowledgement from my government that I could leave a small legacy for my grandchildren and children! I have been honored by many law enforcement agencies throughout this country, but

Page 2

never from the offices of any President or the Federal Government. I am not asking this for myself, even though it would be the greatest honor. It would be for my children and their children, for them to know their government did honor and recognize exceptional deeds that were above and beyond the call of duty by an ordinary cop! I was recognized by my peers and by the City of Dallas and awarded their highest award, the Medal of Honor, which I shall always cherish!

I know that you will be one of our greatest Presidents!

Thank you so much for taking time out of your busy schedule to read my letter. Hopefully, you or your aides will find the time to answer.

Respectfully,

Maurice "Nick" McDonald

(COPY)

To Nick & Daisy
With Appreciation,

*Left: The Medal Of Valor from the National Police Officer's Association of America
Right: Medal Of Honor from the Dallas Police Department*

APPENDIX

1. Tredici, Robert. *At work in the fields of the bomb.* New York: Perennial Library, 1987. 175.

2. Tredici, Robert. *At work in the fields of the bomb.* New York: Perennial Library, 1987. 175.

3. Tredici, Robert. *At work in the fields of the bomb.* New York: Perennial Library, 1987. 84.

4. Lerager, Jim, K. Z. Morgan, and Susan D. Lambert. *In the shadow of the cloud: photographs & histories of America's atomic veterans.* Golden, Colo.: Fulcrum, 1988. 1, 2.

5. Tredici, Robert. *At work in the fields of the bomb.* New York: Perennial Library, 1987. 177.

6. Lerager, Jim, K. Z. Morgan, and Susan D. Lambert. *In the shadow of the cloud: photographs & histories of America's atomic veterans.* Golden, Colo.: Fulcrum, 1988. 114.

7. *Arkansas Democrat-Gazette,* 08 October 1995, sec. 6H.

8. "The Assassination." In *The Warren Commission Report.* New York: Time, 1964. 40.

9. "The Assassination." In *The Warren Commission Report.* New York: Time, 1964. 28.

10. "The Assassination." In *The Warren Commission Report.* New York: Time, 1964. 41.

11. "The Assassination." In *The Warren Commission Report*. New York: Time, 1964. 41.

12. "Detention and Death of Oswald." In *The Warren Commission Report*. New York: Time, 1964. 209-210, 213-215.

13. "Detention and Death of Oswald." In *The Warren Commission Report*. New York: Time, 1964. 215.

14. "Investigation of Possible Conspiracy." In *The Warren Commission Report*. New York: Time, 1964. 352-353, 357.

15. "Investigation of Possible Conspiracy." In *The Warren Commission Report*. New York: Time, 1964. 357.

16. Conversation between Sergeant P.T. Dean and Maurice N. "Nick" McDonald.

17. "Appendix 16: A Biography of Jack Ruby." In *The Warren Commission Report*. New York: Time, 1964. 800.

18. "Appendix 16: A Biography of Jack Ruby." In *The Warren Commission Report*. New York: Time, 1964. 804.

19. "Appendix 16: A Biography of Jack Ruby." In *The Warren Commission Report*. New York: Time, 1964. 805.

20. "Appendix 16: A Biography of Jack Ruby." In *The Warren Commission Report*. New York: Time, 1964. 805.

21. "Appendix 16: A Biography of Jack Ruby." In *The Warren Commission Report*. New York: Time, 1964. 805.

22. "Appendix 16: A Biography of Jack Ruby." In *The Warren Commission Report*. New York: Time, 1964. 805.

23. "Appendix 16: A Biography of Jack Ruby." In *The Warren Commission Report*. New York: Time, 1964. 805.

24. "Appendix 16: A Biography of Jack Ruby." In *The Warren Commission Report*. New York: Time, 1964. 800-801.

25. "Warren Commission Hearings, Volume III." In *The Warren Commission Report*. New York: Time, 1964. 299-301.

26. "Oswald's Arrest." In *The Warren Commission Report*. New York: Time, 1964. 176-179.

27. "The Assassination." In *The Warren Commission Report*. New York: Time, 1964. 49.

28. "The Protection of the President." In *The Warren Commission Report*. New York: Time, 1964. 425.

29. "Appendix VII: A Brief History of Presidential Protection." In *The Warren Commission Report*. New York: Time, 1964. 504-506.

30. Hanchett, William. *The Lincoln murder conspiracies: being an account of the hatred felt by many Americans for President Abraham Lincoln during the Civil War and the first complete examination and refutation of the many theories, hypotheses, and speculations put forward since 1865 concerning those presumed to have aided, abetted, controlled, or directed the murderous act of John Wilkes Booth in Ford's Theater the night of April 14.* Urbana: University of Illinois Press, 1983.

31. Unknown. A note and photos of Boston Corbett were sent to me in the mail (see attached).

32. "Appendix VII: A Brief History of Presidential Protection." In *The Warren Commission Report*. New York: Time, 1964. 507.

33. "Appendix VII: A Brief History of Presidential Protection." In *The Warren Commission Report*. New York: Time, 1964. 508.

34. "Appendix VII: A Brief History of Presidential Protection." In *The Warren Commission Report*. New York: Time, 1964. 508.

35. "Appendix VII: A Brief History of Presidential Protection." In *The Warren Commission Report*. New York: Time, 1964. 509-510.

36. "Appendix VII: A Brief History of Presidential Protection." In *The Warren Commission Report*. New York: Time, 1964. 511.

37. "Appendix VII: A Brief History of Presidential Protection." In *The Warren Commission Report*. New York: Time, 1964. 512.

38. "Appendix VII: A Brief History of Presidential Protection." In *The Warren Commission Report*. New York: Time, 1964. 513.

39. Ford, Gerald R.. *A time to heal: the autobiography of Gerald R. Ford*. New York: Harper & Row, 1979. 309-312.

40. Kelley, Kitty. *Nancy Reagan: the unauthorized biography*. New York: Simon & Schuster, -1991. 327.

41. Wills, Garry. *Reagan's America: innocents at home.* Garden City, N.Y.: Doubleday, 1987. 210-211.

42. Reagan, Maureen. *First father, first daughter: a memoir.* Boston: Little, Brown, 1989. 274.

43. Kelley, Kitty. *Nancy Reagan: the unauthorized biography.* New York: Simon & Schuster, 1991. 331.

44. "Terror on South Lawn." *Newsweek,* September 26, 1994.

45. "Never Safe Enough." *Time,* November 14, 1994.

46. "Summary and Conclusions." In *The Warren Commission Report.* New York: Time, 1964. 1.

47. "Organization of the Motorcade." In *The Warren Commission Report.* New York: Time, 1964. 43.

www.ingramcontent.com/pod-product-compliance
Lightning Source LLC
Chambersburg PA
CBHW020748160426
43192CB00006B/280